LONDON _{as an}
international
business
centre

D1460992

Supporting
UK Businesses

HM Customs and Excise is the Government Department principally responsible for collecting indirect taxes:

- Value Added Tax (VAT);
- Insurance Premium Tax;
- Environmental Taxes (Landfill Tax and Climate Change Levy); and
- Excise duties including Air Passenger Duty.

And for carrying out a number of functions relating to goods and people crossing our national borders.

In all of this we work very closely with the British Chambers of Commerce and the Small Business Service.

Our aims in supporting businesses:

- To keep regulatory burdens to a minimum whilst ensuring the integrity of our taxes. Fewer burdens mean lower administrative costs for businesses, encouraging business start-up and releasing time and money to promote sales necessary for growth; and
- To provide targeted advice and support to businesses which helps them meet their regulatory obligations.

The support we offer:

We pro-actively support businesses in a number of ways:

- By making early contact with all new VAT registered businesses to offer free seminars; one-to-one advice and trade sector leaflets;
- We have collaborated with the Inland Revenue to produce a 'Starting up in Business' guide and video and we also offer two new customs videos 'Welcome to Customs' and 'Keeping Records and Accounts';
- We run a programme of Business Advice Open days;
- Businesses are now able to render their VAT returns electronically;
- We have a National Advice Service with a one-number lo-cost telephone Helpline; and
- We offer a range of Special Accounting Schemes for VAT (cash accounting; retail schemes; annual accounting etc)

We would be delighted to offer businesses advice, guidance and support. In the first instance contact our National Advice Service from 8am to 8pm Monday to Friday on 0845 010 9000.

Further information about HM Customs and Excise may be found by logging on to our website: www.hmce.gov.uk

HM Customs and Excise

LONDON
as an
international
business
centre

Consultant editor
Roderick Millar

**KOGAN
PAGE**

Published in association with
LONDON *of* CHAMBER
COMMERCE AND INDUSTRY

Every possible effort has been made to ensure that the information contained in this handbook is accurate at the time of going to press, and the publishers cannot accept responsibility for any errors or omissions, however caused. No responsibility for loss or damage occasioned to any person acting or refraining from action as a result of the material in this publication can be accepted by the editor or publishers.

This (2nd) edition published 2002

Apart from any fair dealing for the purposes of research or private study, or criticism or review, as permitted under the Copyright, Designs and Patents Act, 1988, this publication may only be reproduced, stored or transmitted, in any form, or by any means, with the prior permission in writing of the publishers, or in the case of reprographic reproduction in accordance with the terms of licences issued by the Copyright Licensing Agency. Enquiries concerning reproduction outside those terms should be sent to the publishers at the undermentioned address.

Kogan Page Ltd
120 Pentonville Road
London N1 9JN
E-mail:kpinfo@kogan-page.co.uk

© Kogan Page 2002

Thames Valley Map. The topographic relief originated from: Mountain High Maps ® Copyright © 1993 Digital Wisdom Inc.
Infrastructure Map. The road and rail data originated from: GB Maps on CD-ROM/Digital Map Data © Bartholomew.

British Library Cataloguing Data
A CIP record for this book is available from the British Library
ISBN 0 7494 3656 5

Typeset by Saxon Graphics Ltd, Derby
Printed and bound in Great Britain by Bell & Bain Ltd, Glasgow

www.hilton.com/uk

"Where to guv? And don't just say *The Hilton*."

You'll have to be more specific. Because in London 'Hilton' means a selection of eleven hotels offering a choice of styles from international to historic, from town houses to high specification business hotels and from the original grand hotel to the latest lifestyle hotel.

Plus it doesn't stop there. In October 2000, we opened one of the largest residential conference centres in Europe at the Hilton London Metropole with the capacity to hold up to 3,000 delegates. And with London's 'best connected' hotel at Paddington station opening at the end of this year, you are only fifteen minutes from Heathrow on the Heathrow Express.

So whether you're travelling on business or just visiting for pleasure, Hilton in London will definitely have the hotel for you whatever your needs.

For more information, call us on **+44 (0) 207 856 8100** for business or **00800 444 58667 (+1-800 445 8667 from the US)** for leisure. And when you book one of our hotels, just don't forget which one.

Hilton London Hotels.

welcome to **Hilton** time

HOUSTON CONSULTING EUROPE

> ## Number 1 for Europe's Top
> ## Financial Services Organizations

Houston Consulting Europe is the only EU affairs consultancy in Brussels founded on a specialization in financial services policy. Global financial institutions, both in the City and across Europe, use our services to support an effective financial industry voice in Brussels - and as their 'eyes and ears'.

We supply EU-related information, political intelligence and early warning, analysis and advice on all matters affecting the financial services sector. Strategies and action plans, contact programmes, and event management are also key elements of our services.

A quality service that makes a real difference.

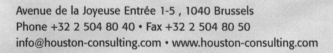

Avenue de la Joyeuse Entrée 1-5 , 1040 Brussels
Phone +32 2 504 80 40 • Fax +32 2 504 80 50
info@houston-consulting.com • www.houston-consulting.com

HOUSTON
CONSULTING
EUROPE

Contents

The Contributors

3i brings capital, knowledge and connections to the creation and development of businesses around the world. It invests in a wide range of opportunities from start-ups to buy-outs and buy-ins, focusing on businesses with high growth potential and strong management. 3i invests in businesses across three continents through local investment teams in Europe, Asia Pacific and the USA. To date, 3i has invested over £13.5 billion (including co-investment funds). In the 12 months to 31 March 2001, an average of £7.8 million (including co-investment funds) was invested each working day. 3i's current portfolio is valued at almost £6 billion.

The Bank of England is the central bank of the United Kingdom, responsible for maintaining the integrity and value of the currency, maintaining the stability of the financial system and ensuring the effectiveness of the UK's financial services. The Bank's Monetary Policy Committee sets UK interest rates.

Geoff Collins is a tax partner in the London office of BKR Haines Watts, one of the top 20 accounting firms in the UK. He is currently chairman of the Taxation Committee of the London Chamber of Commerce and Industry. He specialises in advising start-ups and growing businesses on the full range of tax issues that arise. He has particular experience of helping overseas companies in structuring their inward investments into the UK.

Andrew Cooke is executive director business development at London First Centre, the inward investment agency for the capital. London First Centre is a private and public sector partnership supported by the London Development Agency, Invest.UK (part of the Department of Trade and Industry and the Foreign and Commonwealth Office), and the Corporation of London. In six years of operation, London First Centre's free consultancy service has directly assisted over 500 companies from 32 companies around the world to locate or expand in the capital.

The Corporation of London provides local government services for the financial and commercial heart of Britain, the City of London. Its prime role is to support and promote the City. Its services sustain the City's 24-hour operational needs and its strategic economic development positions the City for the future. It is continually seeking opportunities to ensure the City continues to thrive as the world's leading finance centre and Europe's financial capital.

Jonathan Exten-Wright is a partner in the Employment Department of the City office of the law firm DLA. He practices in all areas of employment on behalf of public and private companies, from the giving of advice at the outset of the employment relationship through to termination on both contentious and non-contentious issues including discrimination. He is a regular seminar speaker and writes articles for various journals. He was a member of the TUPE Forum in dialogue with the Government on reforming business transfer legislation. He also participates in the work of the Disability Partnership. **Mary Walsh** qualified as an assistant solicitor in September 2001 and also works in the employment department at DLA.

The London Communications Agency is the only corporate communications specialising solely on London. The company acts for a number of developers, transport operators and London organisations advising on media relations, public affairs and marketing.

Justina Hurley is Public Relations Manager for DHL International UK Ltd. DHL in the UK is part of DHL Worldwide Express, the leading global air express company with offices in over 228 countries. DHL employs in excess of 65,000 people and runs a fleet of 262 aircraft worldwide.

John Houston is the founder and chief executive of Houston Consulting Europe, a Brussels-based company specialising in EU financial services policy issues.

Houston Consulting Europe is the market leader in Brussels in the supply of information and consulting services to the financial services sector on EU affairs. For more information on our services, see our webpage at www.houston-consulting.com or contact us.

ISIS London and South East is funded by member schools to provide a service to parents who are interested in an independent school education for their children. We have personal experience of independent schools – as past pupils, teachers, governors, admissions officers and parents. We represent every accredited independent school in the region and so are in the unique position of being able to offer unbiased, objective advice.

Catherine Jones is a West End office market analyst for King Sturge, a firm of international property consultants. Following graduation from Durham University in 1998, with a degree in geography, Catherine Jones worked as a portfolio analyst for IPD on secondment. Since June 2000 she has been responsible for the West End of London office market research where she works with both the research and office teams to produce a quarterly market bulletin. In addition, she also carries out *ad hoc* research into a variety of issues including market trend identification, tracking occupier movement and forecasting.

London Chamber of Commerce and Industry is the largest business organisation in the capital with more than 3000 member companies together employing some 500,000 people.

Management Consultancies Association (MCA) was formed in 1956 and represents the leading UK-based consulting firms, which currently employ over 20,000 consultants and generate nearly £4bn in annual fee income. MCA members work for over 90 per cent of the top FTSE 300 companies and all government departments. Management consultancy is an increasingly important industry for the UK economy with revenues for 2000 estimated at £7bn, contributing £1bn to the UK balance of payments.

Manpower Inc. is a world leader in the staffing industry, providing workforce management services and solutions to customers through 3700 offices in 59 countries. The company employs 2.7 million people world-wide each year and is an industry leader in staff assessment and training. Manpower UK is a key part of the manpower network, providing customers with a highly skilled, flexible and productive workforce that can respond to a wide range of business needs. It works with business, government and unions to provide work for around 100,000 people each year. Their approach to employment services includes on-line web-enabled training and job search. Through its website www.manpoweronline.net, the company offers all its staff access to over 1500 training courses in its Global Learning Centre, in subjects as diverse as leadership, communication and customer service, as well as a wide range of IT skills.

Roderick Millar is an experienced writer on business practice and development. He has particular experience of London having run his own business there for the last four years. Roderick was consultant editor for the first edition of this guide as well as to guides to international trade and various editions of the 'Doing Business with ...' series.

Dirk Paterson was recruited by the London Chamber from human rights NGO Christian Solidarity Worldwide, where he has built an impressive profile for the organisation in Westminster over the past two years. Experienced in public relations in a variety of organisations, Paterson's background also includes lobbying on employment issues for the European Youth Forum in Brussels during the UK Presidency in 1998. He has also worked as Research Assistant to Andrew Rowe MP.

Starting a Business?

Running a Payroll?

Help is available from the Inland Revenue.

The **Inland Revenue Business Support Team** will help you to understand
- what records to keep
- what returns to make
- when to send information.

Customers are delighted

96% of our customers tell us they are more confident about running their payroll after receiving our help.

Here is a small sample of customers' comments

'I am actually looking forward to filling in my tax returns – before it seemed very daunting'

'I am now confident thanks to the sessions with the Business Support Team'

'Excellent service, prompt, courteous, competent, helped sort out our payroll mess'

London Business Support Team
Helping Businesses to Get it Right

To find out how we can help you
telephone us on   **020 7667 4830**
e-mail us on   **BST.London@ir.gsi.gov.uk**
Fax us on **020 7667 4825**

INLAND REVENUE

SUPPORTING BUSINESS IN LONDON

Obligations

All businesses have obligations to the Government and its Departments
There are records to keep, returns and payments to make.
This need not be a burden, be too confusing, or difficult to understand.

Help

Help is available to businesses to understand what records to keep, when returns will be due and when to submit information.

This help is designed with businesses in mind, to reassure them that they understand their responsibilities to the Inland Revenue, give them confidence that they are doing the right things and enable them to get on with what they really want to do – make a success of their business.

Business Support Teams

The Inland Revenue has Business Support Teams throughout the UK. There is a Business Support Team which is dedicated to helping the businesses in London. Specially trained Business Advisors offer help in two main ways, through face to face consultations or workshops on specific topics.

The face to face consultations can be held at your business premises. The Business Advisor will discuss with you the Inland Revenue issues about which you feel you would like more information or where you would like an explanation of what you have to do. They will advise you what records you should keep and when you have to send in information.

Workshops are a good way to ensure that you remember information. They are run in small groups of people in similar situations to your own. You will learn about a specific topic, you will be able to practise some examples and you will have reference material to take away with you.

There are 12 distinct workshop topics at the moment but we are adding additional subjects regularly, the number will soon increase to 15. The subjects range from very simple records for those starting in business, what to do when you take on employees, how to pay Statutory Sick Pay, through to calculating National Insurance Contributions for Directors and paying expenses and benefits to your employees. There is also help on paying Tax Credits and the Construction Industry Scheme.

Where to get Help

Look out for the Inland Revenue Business Support Team Advertisement in this publication.

THE LONDON BUSINESS SUPPORT TEAM IS HERE TO HELP YOU.

161 Tottenham
Court Road
London W1T 9NN
Tel: 0207 209 4488

120 High Street
Uxbridge UB8 1JT
Tel: 01895 237330

Colnbrook Bypass
Colnbrook
Slough SL3 0EH
Tel: 01753 680011

American Style Gentlemen's Club with Female Entertainment

OPEN DAILY
FROM 11.00AM

SPEARMINT RHINO

Nationwide
HYGIENE SUPPLIES LTD

The 15 year success story of Nationwide Hygiene Supplies owes a lot to the individual members having a personal stake and therefore a total commitment to the business. Today the company is we believe the strongest independent distributor of hygiene and cleaning supplies.

from strength to strength

A few facts that support our reputation for service:

Annual turnover	£65 million
Field sales personnel	122
Total employees	545
Number of depots	33
Delivery vehicles	125
Customers served	40,000 +
Stock on hand	£5.5 million
Average delivery days	Less than 2 days

You'll find that we're in a 'NATIONWIDE' league of our own!

CALL OUR HEAD OFFICE ON 020 8941 9794

FOR DETAILS OF YOUR LOCAL BRANCH

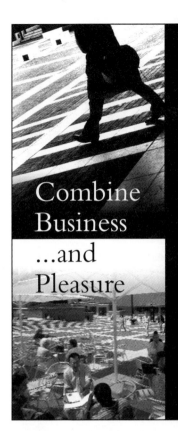

Combine
Business
...and
Pleasure

THE BRITISH LIBRARY

For your work, we offer:

- one of London's newest venues for conferences and meetings
- the most comprehensive business information resource in the UK
- a unique collection of market research reports and journals
- British Library Lloyds TSB Business Line for free enquiries about products, markets and companies
- training courses to help you identify and use business information sources effectively.

And for relaxation:

- exhibition galleries with the nation's Treasures - from Magna Carta to Beatles' manuscripts
- evening events programme to suit all tastes
- a meeting ground for friends and colleagues.

The British Library 96 Euston Rd London NW1 2DB
www.bl.uk 020 7412 7468

Foreword

London is unique. It has consistently been one of the leading global business locations for the last eight centuries. Throughout this time London has had to constantly adapt and re-invent itself to remain a magnet for capital and ability. Now, at the beginning of the twenty-first century it remains Europe's financial capital.

The creation of the Greater London Authority and of London's first directly elected Mayor in May 2000 has given Europe's most successful city a unified tier of democratic self-government once again. Critical to this are two organisations set up under the GLA to tackle some of the more enduring problems it has experienced. *Transport for London* is the new body responsible for delivering an integrated and sustainable transport strategy and the *London Development Agency* has responsibility for formulating and delivering economic development and regeneration across the city. Through them and the other work of the GLA we hope to create an even better business environment to foster growth and economic benefit for all.

London's economy has enormous breadth and depth, reaching over £125 billion in 1999. From the powerhouse of its financial services industry to its world class, but often under appreciated, manufacturing sector London can provide just about any service or product that could be wanted. With Europe's best international transport links and an enviable arts and media industry (which adds over £7 billion to London GDP each year alone) not to mention its world famous sports events, football clubs and its parks and gardens, London is also a very exciting place to live, as well as work.

However, as is to be expected of a city of over 7 million people (and growing), understanding how it works and discovering where to go for assistance can be a complex, sometimes baffling task. This guide, *London as an International Business Centre*, provides a useful introduction to London's business environment and provides clear practical information on how to take advantage of the many commercial opportunities that London offers. I can strongly recommend it to all those considering furthering their business with a London location.

Ken Livingstone
Mayor of London

Appointments Bi-Language

Appointments Bi-Language supply international businesses throughout London & overseas with better educated, better qualified & more versatile support staff.

We are now recognised as a strong supplier of all secretarial & support positions. Our main strengths lie in the banking & finance sector where we supply the majority of the top international banks with both multilingual & monolingual secretaries.

Other clients we work with include companies from the Media, Telecoms, Publishing, Luxury, Leisure & Retail Industries. We have also recently set up a new Legal Division servicing top city law firms.

Appointments Bi-Language

143 Long Acre
London WC2E 9AD
Tel: 020 7836 7878
Fax: 020 7836 7615
www.appointmentsbilanguage.co.uk

Sadler's Wells

Sadler's Wells Theatre

- Modern and flexible auditorium
- Ideal for Awards Ceremonies and Product Launches
- Conferences/AGM's for up to 1500 people
- Gala dinners for up to 500 people

Lillian Baylis Theatre

- Excellent for meetings/workshops/seminars
- Caters for up to 200 people

The Gallery Foyers

- Stylish venue – contemporary artworks
- Wonderfully suited for reception/product launches
- Holds up to 500 people

Sadler's Wells is a fully accessible venue. For more information please contact the Events Department

Sadler's Wells, Rosebury Avenue London EC1 4TN
Tel 020-7863-8065, Fax 020-7863-8199
Email:- events@sadlerswells.com, www.sadlerswells.com

GLAZIERS HALL is a Georgian listed building dated from 1808, situated on the bank of the River Thames alongside London Bridge. This historical Livery Hall features superb views across the River to the City of London.

Centrally positioned, this versatile venue provides the ideal location for conferences, exhibitions and financial events for 10 to 350 delegates. The Banqueting Hall, River Room, Court Room, Library and Masters Room are available in a variety of permutations and work well individually or as syndicates.

For receptions up to 700, and dinners and weddings up to 250 guests, Glaziers Hall offers a unique and elegant setting. Dancing is welcome.

Catering arrangements are extremely flexible, you may select from the list of recommended caterers, who all cater to a high standard, or alternatively use your own preferred caterer.

The friendly and professional sales team understands the importance of your event and is happy to advise on all matters to ensure it is a success.

**Glaziers Hall, 9 Montague Close,
London Bridge, London SE1 9DD.
Telephone: 020 7403 3300   Facsimile: 020 7407 6036
e-mail: sales@glaziershall.co.uk   www.glaziershall.co.uk**

NIGHTFLIGHT INTERNATIONAL

UK & WORLDWIDE EXPRESS

TEL: 020-7820 1111
(24 Hours)

SPECIALISING IN WORLDWIDE EXPRESS DELIVERIES OF DOCUMENTS AND PARCELS DOOR TO DOOR

USA – Nextday – **Cut Off 16:00 Hrs**

NEW YORK CITY – 09:00am, Noon – **Cut Off 16:00 Hrs**

NEW YORK CITY – Nextday – **Cut Off 23:00 Hrs**

HONG KONG/SINGAPORE – Nextday/2 Day

EUROPE – Sameday, 09:00am, Noon & Nextday

UK OVERNIGHT – Timed Deliveries – **Cut Off 20:00 Hrs**

UK SAMEDAY – All Major Cities

CUSTOMER SERVICES & COLLECTIONS 24 HOURS A DAY

Bookings/Track & Trace On-Line at
www.nightflightinternational.co.uk

"Global Strength, Personal Touch"

**Units N103-104, Westminster Business Square
1-45 Durham Street, London SE11 5JH**

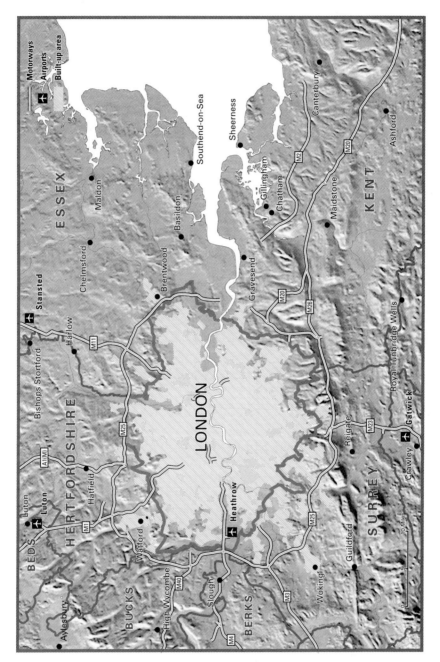

The Thames Valley

The London Boroughs

London Neighbourhoods

London's Neighbourhoods – Key

1	Barnes	large family houses with village atmosphere – expensive
2	Battersea	upwardly mobile district, close to Chelsea, with small houses and many flats – not as cheap as it was
3	Bayswater	mix of crowded flats of Australians and grand apartments owned by foreign businessmen
4	Blackheath	large, spacious family houses and the world's oldest golf club
5	Camden	arty, non-conformist young residential with broad cosmopolitan mix of houses and services
6	Chiswick	grown-up, stable neighbourhood close to M4 so that easy escapes to the country can be made at the weekend
7	City of London	Europe's financial centre – flats in the Barbican Centre but no real 'living-space'
8	Clapham	young families who can't afford Chelsea
9	Docklands	never quite made it as mainstream residential – trendy warehouse conversions and small bachelor apartments
10	Dulwich	the Chiswick of south London – with a famous boys school
11	Fulham	the first flat territory for young professionals – safe but unexciting
12	Greenwich	the site of the Millennium Dome
13	Hammersmith	terraced houses in thriving cosmopolitan area – a good mix of everyone
14	Hampstead	the preferred choice of the art and film world – even the local MP has an Oscar (Glenda Jackson)
15	Highgate	half-way between Camden and Islington in every sense
16	Holborn/Farringdon	law courts and law chambers make this an area of old-fashioned urbanity
17	Islington	New Labour's natural heartland – professionals with a social conscience and an eye for culture
18	Kensington	old conservatism mixed with haute couture fashion boutiques and rich ex-pat Europeans and Americans
19	Knightsbridge/Chelsea	trendy shopping amidst extravagant housing – desirable
20	Maida Vale	around the canal is very picturesque, peaceful
21	Marylebone	embassies and grand apartment blocks to the east and cheaper accommodation in the west by A40 motorway
22	Notting Hill	the culture power-brokers have moved in and made Notting Hill a centre for new style living
23	Pimlico	little atmosphere amongst the white, stucco elegance – the quiet before the storm of Westminster and the West End?
24	Putney	the start of the Oxford vs Cambridge Boat Race indicates the traditional nature of this pleasant area
25	Richmond	spacious houses and small town atmosphere – considers itself outside London
26	Shepherd's Bush	the home of BBC TV with a similar mix of high standards and values but backed by too little money
27	St. John's Wood	known for its large houses and high Rolls Royce ownership
28	Wapping	famous for its newspaper union battles of the early 80s – it is the wrong side of the City to have made it
29	West End	Theatre Land and Mayfair make this area either too exciting or too expensive for any Britons to be able to live here
30	Westminster	MPs' flats and top civil servants amongst the government buildings keep this area in the public eye
A	Hampstead Heath	
B	Hyde Park	
C	Regent's Park	

Part 1

Overview of London's Position

1.1

London – Europe's Global City

Andrew Cooke, London First Centre

London is the leading destination for inward investment in Europe, by far outstripping other European cities in attracting companies from all over the world. The chosen gateway to Europe for business, London offers a powerful combination of a dynamic business environment and a vibrant, cosmopolitan culture.

Major survey results attest London's status as the undisputed business capital of Europe. Ernst and Young's European Investment Monitor reveals that London attracted nearly twice as many investors as Paris during 2000, gaining a quarter share of all new investment in Europe. The Healey & Baker European Cities Monitor, surveying 504 of Europe's largest companies, has ranked London Europe's best business city for eleven consecutive years. London also led the field for the third year running in *Fortune Magazine*'s Best Cities Survey for 2000.

London's inward investment agency, London First Centre, promotes the capital around the world, providing a free and confidential consultancy service to companies considering London as a business location. In six years of operation, London First Centre has helped over 500 companies from 32 countries to locate or expand in the UK capital.

A foremost draw for all investors, regardless of their origin or sector, is London's unrivalled strength as a world financial centre and Europe's business hub. Over 550 foreign banks are located in the capital, more than in any other city in the world. Over 65 per cent of the Fortune Global 500 companies are represented here. Access to all the major global markets, as well as venture capital and investor activity, score highly, as does London's strong professional services sector.

When asked about London's leading edge, investors cite its entrepreneurial spirit and pro-business environment. The ease with which companies can set up in London and the UK's favourable tax and employment legislation are also attractive to companies. Investors speak of a 'can do' attitude and a lack of obstructive bureaucracy.

London's appeal is enhanced by the continued availability of appropriate new buildings and space for development as the public and private sectors collaborate and take initiative in regeneration. Canary Wharf continues to attract the world's leading banks as Lehman Brothers establish their European investment banking headquarters alongside HSBC and Citibank's new towers. International telecoms giant, Orange, is making London the centre of its world-wide operations, relocating staff from Paris and other European cities to a new waterside landmark building at Paddington Basin. The convenience of a 15-minute link to Heathrow, the world's air travel hub, strengthens their choice. London, voted best city for air links (Healey & Baker), is the obvious European headquarters base for international companies.

Language is as crucial as ease of international travel for business investors. They consistently cite the benefit of communication through English, the international business language, as a key reason to favour London over other cities. Language familiarity makes London the obvious bridgehead into Europe for investors from the English-speaking world. London excels in the range of other languages spoken and the availability of multilingual staff, making it the most favoured location for pan-European call centres. Over three hundred languages are spoken in the capital and investors are often impressed with the capital's capacity for rare bilingual skills. A Scandinavian online bookseller, for example, found London could readily provide staff fluent in both Danish and Arabic.

London is renowned as an international centre of research, with 40 universities contributing strongly to the capital's business life and culture. Familiarity with London from student days often influences future senior executives to return with their businesses. The wealth of higher education supplies business with outstanding graduate recruits and is key to London's standing as a world-class ideas and information exchange and the leading skills base for science and engineering. London's knowledge-driven economy and status as a world-class location depend on a highly-developed skills base. The city's long-held position as the international capital of publishing, media and broadcasting brings outstanding skills in marketing and creative design. Voted first in Europe for the availability of qualified staff (Healey & Baker), London has 324,000 IT professionals and 680,000 are employed in the knowledge-driven industries (Annual Employment Survey 1999). Britain offers one of the world's most computer and internet-literate workforces, of whom 45 per cent have access to the Internet.

An unsurpassed entertainment, telecommunications and broadcasting infrastructure supports the talents of London's skilled professionals.

Ranked first for quality of telecommunications, London offers one of the most technologically-advanced infrastructures in the world and is Europe's digital capital. Two-thirds of London businesses have a website, proportionately far more than in the US, Canada, Germany or Japan. Britain has embraced working on the web faster than any European counterpart, making business in London even more attractive for the many companies now focused on e-commerce. Recent e-business investors assisted by London First Centre include Intervisual from Canada, which has set up an office in Brick Lane, East London, and German-owned Cassiopeia, which is based in Euston, North London.

The opportunities in London to enjoy a vibrant social life, excellence across the spectrum of the arts and relaxing recreation, are a strong incentive as companies take increasingly seriously the quality of life of their staff when considering relocation. London's range of communities and enriching diversity of cultures make the UK capital a global city, accessible and adaptable to all cultures, with 25 per cent of the city's population born outside the UK. London is home to at least 37 different communities of over 10,000 originating outside the UK. Investors find the culture, places of worship, arts, language and food of home, as well as thriving community schools. The dynamic, global culture and access to authentic cuisine and arts from almost every nation make London an exciting and creative city in which to work and relax.

London's world-class arts and heritage are renowned world-wide. Thanks to investment and initiative for the new Millennium, the capital's new attractions are drawing record numbers of visitors. Tate Modern, the international art success, and the British Airways London Eye are acclaimed throughout the world. Major refurbishment is transforming the Albert Hall and London Coliseum, alongside the reopened Royal Opera House, rejuvenating London's concert and opera venues in the new century. Two hundred theatres across London present entertainment reflecting the energy and wide cultural offering of a cosmopolitan city from West End musicals to innovative theatre and dance. Investors often praise the enlivening and sophisticated nightlife which brings them back to the office inspired and energised!

Parks and green places make up nearly 30 per cent of London's total area. The Royal Parks offer peaceful enjoyment, recreation and entertainment to those who use them and London's waterways are increasingly enjoyed for sport and leisure. They are joined by new conservation areas such as the Barnes Wetlands project and new cycle links.

All these factors combine to contribute to a strong package of benefits and an unparalleled horizon of choice, attracting an ever-growing community of international businesses to London. They come to take advantage of the city's vast commercial and cultural resources, its sophisticated networks and unrivalled pool of talent and expertise.

For more information, please contact:
Andrew Cooke
Executive Director Business Development
London First Centre
Tel: +44 (0) 20 7925 2000
Fax: +44 (0) 20 7925 2022
Email: acooke@lfc.co.uk
Website: www.lfc.co.uk

1.2

The London Economy – An Overview

Paul Valentine, London Chamber of Commerce

A brief historical introduction

During the 1970s, the decade when inflation threatened to stifle the global economy and when fashion ensured that old wedding photos cannot be viewed without gales of laughter, London's population fell by almost 10 per cent. At its pre-WWII peak, the city had had more than 8½ million inhabitants, but the decline had been so inexorable that few people would have predicted that the 1983 population of 6¾ million – the smallest since Edwardian times – would turn out to be the low point.

Today, there are around 7.5 million people living in London, and the city has recovered a vibrancy that seemed to have been lost forever a quarter of a century ago. There are many reasons for this, but one of the major factors driving population growth has been a buoyant economy, especially over recent years. This chapter will attempt to explain the background to this buoyancy, to detail the circumstances from which it arose, and to make some predictions as to what the future holds.

It is not the intention to suggest that the GLC – the Greater London Council – in any way contributed to the fall in the population of London. However, it is curious how the life of the GLC, which was born in the early 1960s and which died in the mid 1980s, so neatly parallels the downturn in the city's economy. What really harmed London during that quarter of a century was a perception that de-centralisation was the way of the future. Head offices began to be relocated away from London, frequently – though coincidentally, of course – to within a few miles of the chairman's country house, and the combination of high property prices in the capital and substantial relocation packages made it appear that London was in terminal decline.

It is tempting to conclude that it was the Big Bang in 1986, when the de-regulation of the financial markets commenced, that marked the turning point for London's fortunes. Tempting, but wrong since the recovery actually started a couple of years earlier. If there was one factor causing this to happen, it was the discovery by the companies that had relocated out of London that distance from transport, communications and population hubs carried a cost, in terms of both finance and convenience.

Attracting new staff to remote areas proved to be more difficult than expected: not everyone wants to be able to get to the golf course for nine holes before dusk and for younger people, especially, the buzz that cities the size of London create turned out to be hard to replicate in Lower (or even Upper) Snoring. It was not so much that everyone surged back into the metropolis, more that the flood of migrants slowed to a trickle.

Between 1974 and 1981, the UK economy passed through two major recessions. Total GDP grew by just 6 per cent over the period (for comparison, growth over the last eight years has been 26 per cent, more than four times as much). However, despite its falling population, London actually suffered less than other regions, the brunt of the agony being felt by the production industries, especially those in the heavy manufacturing sector (mining, steel, shipbuilding) which were primarily situated in the north of England, Wales and Scotland. Strictly, the recession ended in the second half of 1981, but recovery did not truly start for another year or more. The early seeds of London's economic renaissance were therefore sown by national rather than purely local factors.

Be that as it may, by the middle of the 1980s, London's economic growth rate was back to that of the rest of the UK (see Figure 1.2.1). There was a curious lapse in 1986 but, following the Big Bang at the

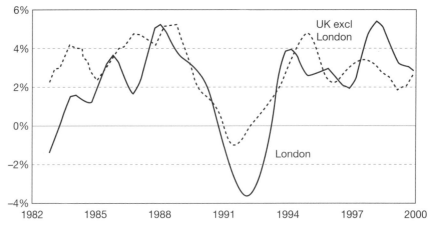

Figure 1.2.1   *Real % change in GDP – London vs UK excl London*
Source: ONS/NIESR

end of that year, the city outgrew other UK regions for the first time for almost a decade.

The first signs of a slowdown in the global economy in the late 1980s were seen in the financial markets, already groggy from the crash of October 1987. London, where although the output of the financial sector is relatively small – around 7 per cent of the total – its influence is large, both noticed this sooner than the rest of the UK and was affected more deeply and prolongedly.

It was not until 1994 that London's growth rate again overtook that of other regions, since when output has risen by 22 per cent against a UK increase of 14 per cent. This has led to speculation that the city is running out of capacity in terms of its resources, both human and industrial. However, a measure of the harshness of the early 1990s recession in the capital can be gauged by indexing London and UK GDP to a 1984 base. This shows that, despite the recent surge, it was not until 2000 that London finally staggered past the UK, suggesting that there is scope for further above-average rates of growth.

Fears that London is in danger of running out of resources have validity. London's unemployment rate is either just above (on a claimant count basis) or significantly higher than (on the ILO definition) that of the UK, and there is evidence that too many of those people lack employable workplace skills.

In addition, the strains on public transport, highlighted by the disruption caused to the overground rail system during the winter of 2000/01 following a crash at Hatfield in October 2000, have made one alternative solution to labour shortages more difficult, that of increased commuting from the Home Counties around London.

The final plank in this resources argument is housing. The cost of the average home in London is more than £60,000 above the UK level, a difference only partially compensated by higher salaries. This problem manifests itself most strongly in a shortage of highly skilled but relatively lowly paid workers, such as teachers, nurses and the police. The good news is that the new Mayor has made the provision of low cost housing for these categories of workers one of his primary targets.

London in the early 21st Century

The London economy enters the new century in surprisingly good shape. The most recent official data for London are for 1998, in common with all of the other UK regions. However, work carried out by LERP[1] has concluded that London's economy has been growing strongly over the past couple of years, with increases around one percentage point above those of the UK.

To overcome this dearth of up-to-date official economic data, London Chamber also carries out regular monthly surveys[2] of business opinion across the city. These surveys ask around 400 or so companies each month for their views on prospects for the economy and for their own companies, as well as detailed information on recent output, expectations for the size of their own workforce and plans for future marketing spend.

The results, which are published each month in *The Evening Standard*, are used as input to the regular quarterly forecasts of London's economy made by LERP. Each quarter, a more detailed set of questions is asked about actual sales levels and order books, both for domestic and export business, plans for investment, price pressures and recruitment. The answers to these questions, many of which have been asked since 1990, provide a timely snapshot of opinion and can be very useful in adding flesh to anecdotal skeletons. One example concerns recruitment, data for which appear in Figure 1.2.2.

As can be seen, attempts to recruit remained high even during the dark days of the early 1990s, when almost 50 per cent of survey respondents said they had been in the market for new staff during the preceding quarter. The big difference, of course, was that finding suitable candidates was not a problem then, though it swiftly became one. There has been a slight diminution in difficulty over the past couple of years, but the chances of finding a suitable candidate for a vacancy reasonably quickly remain low.

Given this shortage of suitable staff, it is perhaps as well that although most areas of the economy have been strong, it is household spending that has been driving growth over the past few years. As Figure 1.2.3 shows, household spend as a share of total GDP has been between five

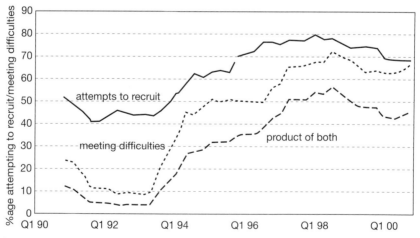

Figure 1.2.2   *Attempts to recruit & meeting difficulties*
Source: LCCI

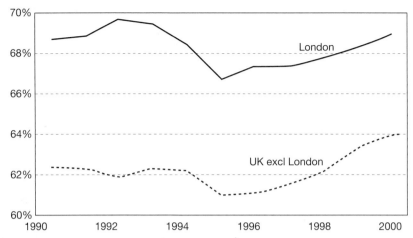

Figure 1.2.3   *Household share of GDP – London vs UK excl London*
Source: ONS/NIESR

and eight percentage points higher in London than in the rest of the UK, and the buoyant nature of this sector has contributed to the city's above-average performance.

The major reason for this, apart from the presence of so many world-class retailers, is the demographic mix of Londoners for, as Figure 1.2.4 shows, London has a significantly younger population mix than the rest of the UK. This difference is particularly strong in the high income/high spending 25–44 year old age group. This reflects both the employment opportunities in London, which tend to favour younger age groups, and also the way in which London, like nearly every capital city, acts as a

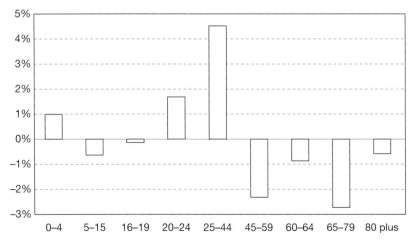

Figure 1.2.4   *Demographics – London vs UK excl London:*
% age point difference by broad age group 1998
Source: ONS/LCCI

magnet for young people in cultural and entertainment terms. (In passing, the excess of women over men is slightly below the national average in London. It would be a foolish (male) author who dared to comment on this fact.)

It could be argued that it is dangerous to rely too much on consumer spending to maintain an economy's health. Admittedly, London's household savings ratio – the difference between income and outgoings – is generally lower than elsewhere in the UK by around one to two percentage points, but this has been an historical reality for many years and is unlikely to change in the short term, especially if the housing market holds up. The latter is used as a proxy for feelings of wealth, and with prices having shot up by 120 per cent over the past five years, twice the UK average rise, it is fair to say that the 56 per cent of Londoners who are owner-occupiers are likely to be feeling pretty well off.

This owner-occupier share is around ten percentage points lower than the UK average, however, and though some of this difference is voluntary as a result of the many city dwellers who choose to rent either for reasons of convenience or because their main home is elsewhere, it also reflects one of the less salubrious aspects of the London economy: the wide divergence of wealth in the city, often in neighbouring areas. The best measure of this is seen in the unemployment data.

In the UK, there are slightly more than 400 unitary and local authority districts for which claimant count data are provided. In late 2000, London had the three local authorities with the worst rates of unemployment in the country – Haringey, Newham and Lewisham – all of which were in excess of 10 per cent. In contrast, thirteen out of the remaining 30 districts had rates which were close to or below 3 per cent, the level at which an economy is considered to have full employment. It has to be allowed that inequality is a feature of all large cities: it could even be argued that it is a necessary condition, since cities need relatively poor people to supply cheap labour, and those people need low cost but reasonably accessible areas in which to live.

There are therefore good historic reasons for this discrepancy in unemployment rates – poor housing, education and transport links, and the departure of large swathes of manufacturing, especially during the 1960s and 1970s – and though the arrival, in July 2000, of an elected Mayor of London promises to provide a focus on these problems, the cheek by jowl existence of areas of great wealth and great poverty is likely to be a feature of London for many years. The shortage of human resources, and the inability of many skilled people to travel to areas of job opportunity, is probably the greatest problem facing London during the early part of the 21st century.

Forecasts for London's economy

In 2000, London's GDP is estimated to have been between £130bn (resident-based) and £150bn (workplace-based), the latter figure taking into account the million or so workers who commute into the city every day. This means that London represents 15½—18 per cent of the total UK GDP, a pretty impressive slice for somewhere whose population share is only just over 12 per cent. (To put this performance into context, the current resident-based share is almost £30bn more than is warranted on a straight population basis.)

This over-representation has its downside, since it means that Londoners contribute far more to the national exchequer – London Chamber and NIESR estimate the figure to be around £20bn annually[3] – than they receive in benefits, but it does emphasise the importance of the city to the nation. The shares of GDP, which fell between the mid 1980s and the early 1990s, are forecast to be around or slightly above their current levels over the medium term.

London's position in global terms is a shifting beast as a result of ever-changing exchange rates. The weakening of the euro against the US dollar has enabled the UK economy to claim fourth place in the world, behind the US, Japan and Germany, and the same effect probably allows London to claim currently to be the sixth largest economy in the EU, though it would be challenged by Belgium and Sweden. In global terms it might, on a good day, scrape into the top 20. Whatever the impact of exchange rates, however, it's a pretty impressive performance for a city of seven million inhabitants.

The primary reasons behind its high share of the UK economy are the productive and earning capacities of London's workers. Average salaries in London are around 40 per cent above the UK level (in the City itself, they're more than double[4]) and annual productivity growth is estimated to have been half a percentage point higher over each of the past four years in London compared to the UK.

Another, though seldom mentioned reason is the unusual relationship between the number of people who are economically active and the number of workforce jobs in London. In nine (out of twelve) UK regions, there are slightly more of the former than the latter. In two other regions, the two figures are similar but in London, there are 15 per cent more jobs than there are economically active people. This readiness (and, to be fair, possibly the necessity) to hold down more than one job at a time is a major reason why the output of London's workforce is so much higher than in other regions.

London's industrial composition

In common with most of the world's capital cities, the businesses that make up London's economy are different from the rest of the country. Figure 1.2.5 gives the latest official data. It is unlikely that the differences between London and the rest of the UK will cause much surprise, agriculture and mining not having featured heavily in the city for centuries if, indeed, ever.

The lifeblood of London, despite taking a lower share than might be expected, is the financial sector which is two and a half times as great as in the rest of the UK. The advantage of looking at shares is that it allows different totals to be compared: the disadvantage is that one sector's gain is inevitably another's loss, but London's relative lack of education, health and social workers is a cause for concern and one that is continually exacerbated by the shortage of affordable housing for these essential staff. It may be useful, however, to say a few words about manufacturing.

It cannot be denied that the sector in London is much smaller than in other regions of the UK. However, manufacturing has staged a successful holding operation in the city over recent years, spearheaded by the Made in London campaign[5] which is a joint initiative of London Chamber of Commerce and the LDA[6], such that employment in the sector has remained steady over the past year despite a fall of over 2 per cent across the rest of the UK. It has done this by concentrating on the growing areas of the economy – light rather than heavy industry – and on products where adding value is more important than producing down to a price.

The five-year forecasts of growth by sector appear in Figure 1.2.6. As can be seen, the race looks like going to the strong which is exactly as

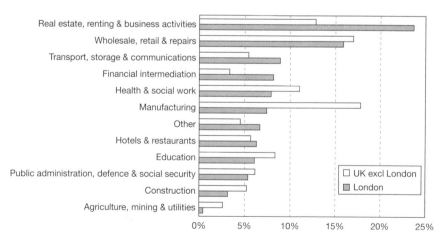

Figure 1.2.5   *Workforce composition 2000 – London vs UK excl London*
Source: Labour Market Trends

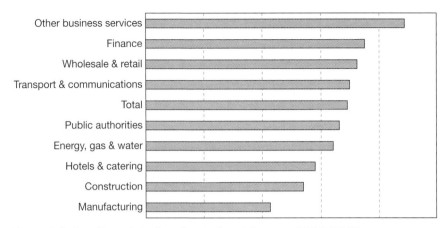

Figure 1.2.6   *Growth by London industrial sector 2000–2005*

one would expect in a city as dynamic as that of London. Two apparently under-performing sectors which deserve brief mention are hotels and catering, and construction. Both are expected to suffer from a hangover from 2000 with a slowdown in tourism growth and the completion of a number of so-called Millennium-inspired projects, respectively, and both will also be victims of the overall shortage of qualified workers referred to earlier.

What next for London?

Most forecasts are extrapolations of the past, infused with a smattering of stability as unviable inconsistencies work their way out of the system. The forecasts in this chapter are no different, and though they are based on sound economic theory and as robust a set of data about London as one could hope to find, dangers nevertheless lurk. This final section will therefore concentrate on potential pitfalls that could waylay the otherwise sunny future.

At the time that this article is being written (January 2001), the obvious threat is the US economy. Nothing lasts for ever, not even plutonium, so no one with a sense of history would have been surprised that, after the longest ever peacetime expansion, the halving of growth between the second and third quarters of 2000 led rapidly to fears that everything was about to go avocado-shaped. As Figure 1.2.7 shows, there is a remarkable correlation between the US and the London economies which is closer than there is between the London and UK economies. This has its upsides – London has benefited from the boom in the US stock market, in particular – but as Manchester City fans are discovering, what goes up fast inevitably comes back down at the same rate.

Figure 1.2.7   *GDP growth – London, UK & US*
Source: ONS/Consensus Forecasts

Of course, the financial market is not the only sector in London that would suffer if the US economy were to crash, but it's likely that it would bear the brunt of the blow. It should be noted that even if the pre-emptive downward move in US interest rates in early 2001 does stave off a crash, it will almost certainly only be temporary. Indeed, it could be argued that by giving the impression that maintaining the level of share prices is the over-riding aim of the US Federal Reserve, when the final crash does occur, it will be even worse than it would otherwise have been.

The other threats to London have already been referred to. They are all internal, and relate to a dearth of resources both of the human variety and in terms of infra-structure. Businesses invariably claim that there is a shortage of skilled staff, even at times of apparently plentiful supply, such as during recessions. Of course, it's impossible to disentangle these claims from both expectations and the readiness to pay, but the time gap between education and application makes it inevitable that there will always be a mismatch between the skills that have been historically taught and the skills that are currently required, lifelong learning skills policy or no lifelong learning skills policy.

This is not a problem confined to London. However, there is a danger that the additional factors of a shortage of reasonable low-, or even mid-price housing, the high price of office accommodation, and the cost of and time involved in commuting into London may combine to stifle the city's growth potential. Hope that this gloomy scenario remains hypothetical springs from two sources: the first-ever elected Mayor of London, Ken Livingstone, who will fight the city's corner after an absence for a decade and a half of a champion, and London's remarkable ability to re-invent itself. It is the latter that underpins the forecast that, by 2005, the size of London's economy will exceed £200bn, a figure that is larger than the total GDP of the world's poorest countries which is 60 per cent [7].

Notes

[1]   the London Economy Research Programme, run by London Chamber and NIESR (the National Institute of Economic and Social Research) with the help of a range of business sponsors

[2]   for further details, contact London Chamber's economist on 020 7203 1882

[3]   for further details, see 'London's contribution to the UK economy', a LERP publication issued by London Chamber in September 2000

[4]   despite weekly hours worked in the City being six per cent *below* the national average

[5]   formerly the London Manufacturing Group

[6]   the London Development Agency

[7]   whether this is something to be proud or ashamed of is left to the reader to decide

1.3
Political Structure

Roderick Millar

The Recent Political Past

'London has always been a muddle'[1]. In the period between 1890 and today London Government has had four significant reorganisations. Meanwhile Paris has only had one and New York has only had one. The latest re-organisation occurred in May 2000. In order to understand its dynamics, it is necessary to have an appreciation of the events that have led to its creation. Yet it is true to say that if you were to devise a political system for a great international city from scratch, it would most likely not bear any resemblance to the multi-layered administration that exists in London today.

London is made up of 32 local borough councils and The Corporation of London. There had been an over-arching administrative body for London since 1888, originally the London County Council and from 1965 the Greater London Council (GLC). By the early 1980s the GLC was run by Ken Livingstone, a young left-wing politician with a radical agenda very much opposed to the national government of Mrs Thatcher. However, having vanquished the miners and brought the unions to heel, Mrs Thatcher's Conservative Government, at the height of its reforming zeal, was in no mood to put up with a socialist power-base administering the centre of London. The Greater London Council was abolished in 1986 and London was centrally governed through the Department of the Environment for the next sixteen years.

With the election of the first Labour government in the UK for eighteen years the country's political structure was to be altered dramatically. In coming to power, Tony Blair had pledged to offer Scotland and Wales the opportunity to organise their own devolved parliament and assembly to make their own domestic laws and procedures. The larger 'national' issues: tax and the economy, foreign affairs and defence would still be decided in London. By 1999 both Scotland and Wales had gained their respective parliament and assembly and the focus had turned to England and how it could benefit from more local democracy. The answer was not very clear, but regional governments and directly elected mayors for the big cities were much talked about.

London was clearly the most needy of reform being the only global city to be run by central government. The GLC was to be reborn, this time under the poorly disguised mantle of the Greater London Authority (GLA). Tony Blair was keen to be seen to be devolving power away from Westminster, but the reality seemed that he wished to be able to pull the strings of power without appearing to be in charge. Each of the major political parties produced a mayoral candidate, but the Labour party managed to tie themselves in knots in the process. It was clear from an early stage that the Labour voting members of the London electorate wanted to have Ken Livingstone as their candidate. Since the abolition of the GLC in 1984 Ken Livingstone had become a Labour MP at Westminster. He had become less of a firebrand activist over the following 16 years but he was still firmly to the left of New Labour's ever more business friendly image. As a result Tony Blair was determined that Mr Livingstone should not become the Labour figurehead in London. A complex electoral college system was devised to choose the Labour party candidate, which appeared to have the sole purpose of stopping Ken Livingstone becoming the mayoral candidate of the Labour party. It worked – to an extent. The rank and file membership overwhelmingly voted for him but were outpaced by the block vote of the MPs and unions. Mr Livingstone, maverick politician that he likes to portray himself as, decided to stand anyway, as an independent candidate. For this he was banished from the Labour party, but the more important consequence was that he was elected to be London's mayor.

All these political manoeuvrings have a relevance. The London mayor and the GLA have only a limited range of powers to cover a broad range of responsibilities. In order to maximise their influence it is essential for them to be able to co-operate with both the local boroughs and with central government, which still has much power. The fact that central government and the mayor's office are antipathetic to each other clearly limits the extent to which new initiatives can be achieved.

The Structures

The Greater London Authority is a new and unique form of strategic citywide government for London. It is made up of a directly elected Mayor – the Mayor of London – and a separately elected Assembly – the London Assembly.

The Mayor is elected every four years by a London wide electorate. He prepares plans on issues from transport to the environment, and from culture to land use, directs the GLA and sets budgets for the GLA, Transport for London, the London Development Agency, the Metropolitan Police and London's fire services.

The Assembly is made up of 25 members, also elected every four years. It scrutinises the Mayor's activities, questioning the Mayor about his decisions. The Assembly is also able to investigate other issues of importance to Londoners, publish its findings and recommendations, and make proposals to the Mayor.

The GLA oversees four functional agencies: Transport for London (TfL), the London Development Agency, the Metropolitan Police and the London Fire and Emergency Planning Authority. The Assembly is elected through a complex constituency basis by a form of proportional representation. It is currently made up by 9 Labour members, 9 Conservative members, 4 Liberal Democrat members and three Greens.

While the GLA has responsibility for London-wide programmes and initiatives, it is the 33 unitary authorities that will probably be the most likely point of government contact with any new business in London. There are 31 London boroughs and two Cities (City of London and City of Westminster) in the Greater London area.

The City of Westminster is essentially the same in structure as all the other boroughs. The City of London however is eccentrically unique. It is the result of over 1000 years of political development in London. The first mayor appeared in 1190 and what is now the Corporation of London has been running and collecting taxes in the City of London, in one form or another ever since. The Corporation operates through its Lord Mayor, 24 other Aldermen and 112 members of the Court of Common Council. The Mayor and Aldermen are elected by the members of the ancient Livery Companies (self-regulating guilds dating back to the medieval period) and the Court is elected by rate payers, whether they be individuals or companies. It works through committees, like any other local authority, but it is unique in that it is non-party political. It is the Lord Mayor of the City of London, in his gilded carriage, robes and tricorn hat, who is often incorrectly perceived as being the mayor of London.

Central government still has a large part to play in London's governance. Although the new authority was created to restore an overall level of regional democracy to the capital, the central government did not return to it all the powers it removed with the abolition of the GLC. A number of government departments still have responsibility for many areas of London's regulation, The Department of Transport, Local Government and the Regions (DTLR) being the most involved. However, the Home Office (for policing), the Department of Culture, Media and Sport (the re-building of Wembley stadium amongst other issues), the Department of Trade and Industry (economic development strategies) and others are all involved. To make this 'muddle' easier to deal with, the Government Office for London (GOL)[2] exists to act as the bridge between central government and the GLA and boroughs.

The Implications

The new layer of London Government has a major challenge ahead to prove its value. The period of sixteen years since the GLC was abolished was also a period when London prospered. Its population started to grow again as its attractiveness to traditional financial businesses and new creative and technology industries increased. It will be critical for the GLA to, at the very least, continue this trend and hopefully to improve on it. But what can the various levels of local government actually do to improve the city's attractiveness?

Government in the UK nowadays plays a much lesser role in the actual functioning of business life than it has done in the past. However, the amount of regulation has continually increased. It is one of the main roles of local government development organisations to smooth the path of new businesses; to ensure the infrastructure is improved and that bureaucratic barriers reduced.

The mayor has focused on a number of key areas where he hopes to make a significant impact. 'In my first year I have had two priorities: establishing the structure of the Greater London Authority, the first executive mayoralty in Britain, as an effective organisation; and putting in place the tough policies necessary to get London back on its feet. I have worked in partnership with other London-wide bodies to put these policies in place.'[3] He has, though, acknowledged that structural changes will take time and that significant improvements may be hard to detect until his (hoped for) second term of office.

For businesses the major impact of the GLA, so far, is probably its focus on improving the transport infrastructure. The issue has not been on whether the Tube requires further investment – it clearly does, but on how it should be paid for. The funding argument on how to improve the London Underground is dealt with in Chapter 2.1, but suffice to say that the Mayor and his New York Commissioner for Transport, Bob Kiley, have spent much of their first year in office fighting with central government against their PPP (Public Private Partnership) initiative in favour of a NYC-style bond issue for the funding. Interestingly, as a possible indication of who holds the upper hand between the new authority and central government, the government has won the battle in the courts. However, only time will show whether PPP is the correct way forward.

The mayor's immediate stated goal 'is to increase and improve bus services with 27 major routes upgraded by April 2002 and lower fares. A 70p flat rate bus fare will be introduced throughout the city. The strategy will:

- increase bus capacity by 40 per cent by 2011;
- increase London Underground and rail capacity by 40 per cent in ten years;
- reduce traffic in central London by 15 per cent, cut traffic growth in inner London to zero and in outer London by a third.'[4]

Beyond transport the mayor is keen to grow the London economy on the strength of its skilled workforce. Funding is now available through the five new Learning and Skills Councils to build on the capital's skills resources. A clear leader in the financial, technology, design and creative industries, with a uniquely high supply of multi-lingual workers – the economy is held back by a bottle-neck at administrative and ancillary levels. The shortages in supply have increased the costs and London consequently appears high up the expense charts for doing business as a result. The new Councils aim to redress this supply deficiency.

In a similar fashion to the above problem, the mayor is very concerned about the supply of cheap housing in central London. The increase in population and income, driven by the successful City economy has sent house prices soaring over the last decade. The average London house now costs nearly £200,000[5], and in the heart of central London considerably more. This is maybe just affordable to well paid executives and City personnel but is prohibitive to 'key workers', such as teachers, nurses and the police. By increasing the level of 'affordable homes' beyond the current 25 per cent of any new housing development the mayor intends to improve the situation. Getting the right balance will be vital and getting more affordable homes essential if London is to retain key workers.

The mayor is the first person for many years in a position to address the issue of the image of London as a whole. The Lord Mayor of London has been an enthusiastic ambassador for the City of London, supported by the Corporation of London. The individual borough mayors have also done much to promote their own areas. But London has suffered from not having itself projected as a single successful entity. The new mayor has addressed this by creating an environment commission to 'consider how the environmental strategies of Waste, Air Quality, Noise, Energy and Biodiversity can best be developed in a holistic manner'. It is a priority to reverse London's image of being dirty and run down.

The mayor has also appointed a Head of London House, the new London office in Brussels, to promote London in Europe and ensure that London benefits from all EU assistance available.

A further expression of the overall responsibility for London is in a new tier of planning approval. While it is not unexpected that the mayor would want to have a role in granting planning permission for large 'strategic' developments, so as to be able to build a coherent development structure across the whole city, it also means that there are now three layers of planning permission to be sought for any major building development – the local borough, central government and now the mayor. This inevitably will lead to longer application procedures and increased costs. Worryingly, as some have noted, the mayor has involved himself in some developments not only on strategic grounds but also questioning the quality of the architecture.[6]

Financial Implications

The main financial burden imposed by local government in London is in the form of 'business rates'. The 'rateable value' of every property, be it office, warehouse, shop is evaluated every five years. The most recent evaluation was in April 2000. The 'rateable value' is based on the expected market rent of the property, usually for a specific date two years before the evaluation. The valuation is carried out by the Valuation Office, a central government agency. Each year central government sets a nationwide 'multiplier' (a percentage figure, 41.6 per cent in 2001) which the local council will multiply against the rateable value to give the tax payable on the property. This maximum figure is then often reduced by specific reliefs available on that property.[7]

For individuals, the system is simpler but less equitable. The local council levies a charge on each household set by the value of the house in April 1991. While the bands for house values are the same across London (and the rest of the country) the charge applied to each band is determined by each council. So someone living in a house which falls in Band G (valued between £160,000 to £320,000) in the Borough of Lambeth would pay £1093 whereas one kilometre away in the Borough of Wandsworth they would pay just £662 a year. The council charge is reset every year.

The GLA gained no power to levy direct taxes when it was created, but it is able to set a 'precept' or additional charge on the local boroughs tax. The GLA has levied a precept in its first year specifically to fund more police on the streets. This extra charge has not endeared the GLA to the local authorities. The most significant new expense that the GLA may be seen to levy is the proposed new 'congestion charge'. The mayor is proposing to charge a fee on all vehicles that enter the centre of London. The current proposed fee is £5 per car per day. The revenue raised from the congestion charge will go directly to improving the public transport infrastructure. This charge is not expected to be in operation until 2003 at the earliest, as it faces many obstacles, both technological and philosophical.

Of course the GLA would not want to give the impression that it is just another layer of expenses. In its defence the mayor keeps a close watch on London's relative position regarding payments to and from central government. Previously nobody was in a position to fight on a united front for London as a whole. At present London pays around £18 billion more to the government than it gets back in grants. The mayor has commented 'I have expressed concern over the estimates of earnings in London which will be used by the government in calculating 2002/2003 grant settlements for local authorities. The DTLR figures which appear to show that earnings in inner London have risen by only 0.1 per cent over a 12 month period, compared to 2.7 per cent in outer London and 4.3 per cent outside of London and the South East. If this 0.1 per cent figure is used in the formula to calculate the grant from central government to the London boroughs and the GLA then the potential loss could be as much as £140million ... London's population continues to rise yet over the last five years we have seen our share of public expenditure fall by £2billion a year. As a result, London's public services are already nearing crisis point. Any further diversion of resources away from the capital would have a disastrous effect not just on London but on the UK's economy as a whole.' By using his role to fight for London as a whole, the mayor keeps the pressure up in central government on the city's behalf.

London has done significantly better from the latest round of EU Objective 2 funding grants than in the past. Gaining £159 million in the recent distribution. The co-ordinated front presented by the GLA played a major part in this. Ken Livingstone is an enthusiastic proponent of the EU, and not just for the funding benefits. He is chairman of the 'London in Europe' campaign and a voluble supporter of the euro.

Conclusion

London's political structure is still a muddle but it is to be hoped that the new GLA will grow to become a useful and strong coordinating body to represent the whole of the city. It still has to prove its worth and if it can deliver results quickly it may well evolve to gain greater powers.

Currently no other UK city has chosen an elected mayor as a suitable way forward, although in a recent survey (September 2001) in Birmingham, over 57 per cent of respondents were in favour of some sort of elected mayor.

Notes

[1] Peter Ackroyd *London – A Biography* pp762
[2] for more information on GOL see: www.go-london.gov.uk

[3] Ken Livingstone, article in The Independent 02/05/01
[4] for more information of the mayor's transport strategy see: www.london.gov.uk/mayor/
[5] see latest price guide at: www.bbc.co.u./rightmoves/
[6] for further information on the planning process see the mayor's website: www.london.gov.uk/mayor/planning_decisions/
[7] for further information see: www. local-regions.detr.gov.uk/rev2000/leaflet/

Part 2

Transport Infrastructure

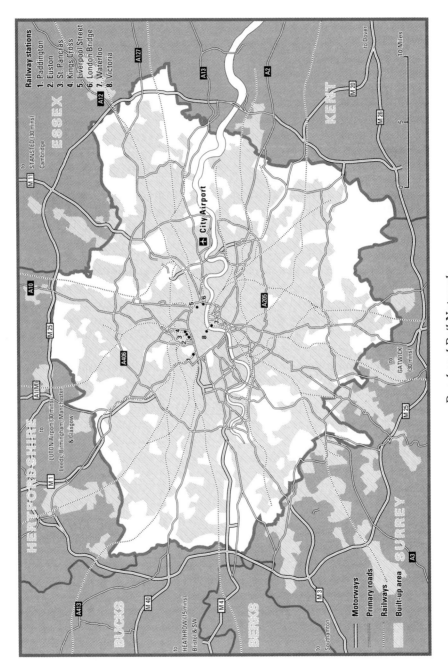

Road and Rail Network

London's Underground – the Tube – carries 3 million people every weekday, putting it at the heart of the city, key to London's position as *the* International Business Centre.

The London Underground is the world's oldest metro. We are as proud of our heritage as we are of the stunning new extension to the Jubilee line, opened in 1999, whose stations have already won many architectural awards.

There is much more investment to come. £13 billion, guaranteed, over the next 15 years as a result of new partnerships with the private sector now being finalised.

Delivering new trains, new track, new signals and new-look stations. Helping to make our excellent safety record better still.

And helping to keep London as the natural choice for business.

To find out more, visit our website at **www.thetube.com**, or call our Public Affairs team on **020 7918 3492**.

www.thetube.com

2.1

Passenger Transport

Dirk Paterson,
London Chamber of Commerce

Transport and politics

The winds of change are blowing over the transport landscape of London. These are winds that bring good tidings for the business which is considering locating in London over the next few years. Transport has had some bad press in London and it became the key focus of the first London Mayor elections in May 2000. Ken Livingstone knows he will be judged primarily over his provision of transport for Londoners. So it is good news for incoming business that he has hitched his wagon to the transport train.

Transport and the growth of the London Economy

'Things can only get better'. As New Labour said of the UK in '97, so Londoners might say of their public transport. But it is worth a closer look at how London really fares on an international scale. Healy and Baker's report on Europe's Top Cities[1] in October 1999 rated London as Number One city in terms of external transport links, and indeed London reached the top position in cities which are 'easy to get around' (i.e. internal transport systems). That is a key reason why London is currently the first choice for many international company sites, 26 per cent of the world's largest companies have their European headquarters in London, 65 per cent of the Fortune Global 500 companies are represented in London and 539 foreign banks have headquarters in London – more than in any other city in the world. London's economy is greater than that of Norway, Poland and Greece; the economy of the South East region amounts to 36 per cent of the country's GDP.

Growth in the economy means growth in public transport demand

In one sense London's transport systems are a victim of the city's own economic success. Employment in London has grown by around 450,000 since 1994. Passenger kilometres both on London Underground and the buses are now higher than in previous peak year of 1988–89. Passenger kilometres travelled on London's entire trans- port network have increased by 20 per cent since 1994. Some 3 million people a day use the underground system – more than the whole of the national rail network. Travel on London's surface rail network has increased by 26 per cent in the five years to 1998/99, amounting to 38 per cent of the total rail travel on the national network.[2] So despite still being the easiest city to get around, under the weight of demand, public transport has slipped a little. The average rush-hour traffic speeds in London are now at comparable levels to those at the start of last century, so there is room for improvement.

The state of the Tube

Perhaps the most contentious area of London travel life is the London Underground. Although suffering from bad press, the London Underground is a network which provides a near comprehensive service in Central London. Other than New York it is the largest metro network in the world with 253 stations and over 180 kilometres of tunnel. If a business were to locate within Central London it could be assumed that the majority of its workforce would use this facility. Having said that, 60 per cent of London's population use the Tube less than once a month – this is due to the growing population who live and work in London's suburbs.[3] It provides a service for 18 million different customers every year, in addition to the 1.2 million (1.2m is the total number of people entering Central London during morning rush hour; about half of these will use the Tube for all or part of their journey) who use the Tube to travel into work every day. The daily service runs from around 5.30 am until midnight, when it is replaced by a night bus service, which operates a skeletal service till the Tube restarts.

There has, in recent years, been some uncertainty about the future of the Tube. There have been many years of under-investment and stop-start funding under successive governments of different political colours, resulting in a massive backlog of work that needs doing to upgrade the infrastructure. The new arrangements for managing transport in London have, initially, complicated matters. The GLA (Greater London Authority) is made up of the newly elected Mayor, and the separately elected Assembly. Transport for London is the executive body in the GLA which is responsible for London's transport. However the system is not wholly in the hands of the Mayor yet. The government was eager to set up a private funding scheme for the tube in advance of releasing the tube to the Mayor, but the PPP (Public Private Partnership) scheme is viewed with great suspicion by the Mayor and by his New Yorker Commissioner for Transport, Bob Kiley. They stand to inherit a system which they will be required to run within a structure they oppose. Lengthy talks between John Prescott – at the time Secretary of State for the Department of Environment, Transport and the Regions – and Mr Kiley, followed by a period of direct negotiation between Mr Kiley and the consortia bidding for the PPP contracts, when he was temporarily Chairman of the Tube's holding company, London Transport, have failed fully to resolve the points at issue.

There are two essential concerns put forward by Mr Kiley. The first is that the funding proposals will be expensive, because of the borrowing rate from private sector money, the second being that the arrangement would necessitate the dividing up of the current system such that maintenance/upgrading of the infrastructure on different lines would be managed by different departments. The Underground's main trade unions are also opposed to the scheme and have taken industrial action, on the grounds that the scheme would compromise safety standards.

The Tube's managers, for their part, are keen to get on with the task of injecting money into the system. Now that a legal challenge to the scheme by Mr Kiley and Mr Livingstone has failed, it looks as though the way is clear for them to do so, once contracts for the three infrastructure companies have been finalised. Responsibility for running all the Tube lines – driving the trains, operating the stations and the signals – will remain in the public sector with London Underground.

Further delay and disruption, the business community advises decision makers, is to be avoided. Disruption can cause a loss of up to £50 million for London business in any one day. Controversy aside, tube customers seem to be reasonably satisfied with the service they are being given. The volume of train service operated rose by 1 per cent last year and record numbers of people are using the service – around one billion in 2000/2001. Measures of customer satisfaction show healthy results – 75 per cent profess satisfaction with the train service, for example – although these results are not at a high enough level to meet the demanding targets set by the government.

So is the Tube reliable? The system is certainly showing its age. In 2000/2001 the average excess journey time – in effect, the average delay experienced by customers – was 3.69 minutes, a deterioration from 3.19 minutes the previous year. London Underground aim to bring this figure down through a co-ordinated programme of measures to improve reliability, but the fact is inescapable that many delays result from the failure of ageing assets.

When it comes to the Tube, the system is the talk of Londoners. Londoners love and hate the Tube. They marvel at the drama of the new Jubilee Line stations as they rise from the ground in nouveau art deco grandeur, they smile affectionately at the well kept gardens on the Metropolitan Line, they stare at each other over the top of their newspapers or from under one another's armpits on a busy rush hour. They read 'poems on the underground', they listen reverently to the infinite variety of buskers and complain bitterly when 'leaves on the line' is announced on the tannoy as the reason they are late.

'Things can only get better' they may say. Statistically there is scope for them to get much worse, but they will not. The Tube has a massive investment programme in one form or another ahead of it. We expect to see the systematic upgrading of stations; extensions to lines including the East London Line extension; increased train frequency following the completion of track and signalling works; a smart card ticketing system to speed up journeys; replaced escalators and lifts; new and refurbished trains; CCTV in 58 Tube car parks; interchanges with other transport modes by extending cycle facilities, taxi ranks and other transport links. After the uncertainty, the future now looks bright.

Fares/tickets

It has a reputation for being an expensive system to use. The system is organised in zones 1 to 6 with prices for tickets paid per zone. These tickets can be used also on the bus and the light railway network. Adult single fares are £1.50 for one zone, £1.90 for two zones, £2.20 for three zones, £2.70 for four zones, £3.30 for five zones and £3.60 for six zones of travel. These fares are doubled for a return ticket. There are various reductions. Open one day travel cards which offer unlimited travel between the stated zones when purchased after 09.30; for £4.00, zone 1 and 2; £4.30, zones 1,2,3 and 4; £4.90, zones 1,2,3,4,5 and 6 with a flat rate for children of £2. Similarly a weekend travel card offers a 25 per cent cheaper fare than two separate one day travel cards and allows travel on consecutive days or public holidays with a flat rate for children of £3. There is also a reduced rate for family travel cards. Seasonal travel cards offer further reductions with a weekly rate of £15.90, monthly rate of £61.10, annual rate of £636 for zone 1; weekly rate of £18.90, monthly rate of £72.60, annual rate of £756 for zones 1 and 2; £22.40, £86.10 and £896, for zones 1,2 and 3; £27.60, £106 and £1104 for zones 1,2,3 and 4; £33.30, £127.90 and £1332 for zones 1 to 5 and £36.40, £139.80 and £1456 for zones 1 to 6.

Buses

The London Bus is something of an icon of transport affection all over the world. It also carries four million people a day in London – more than all English metropolitan areas combined. Where the London traveller cannot reach a location by Tube, they will generally have access by London Bus. London Buses are having something of a renaissance. In short, Ken Livingstone loves the London Bus and sees it as taking some of the capacity strain from the Tube. The bus has dropped in popularity over the past twenty years whilst the Tube has become a great deal more popular. This is going to require a fundamental modal shift in attitude, as the bus is not really regarded as a business transport option.

To counter this there has been a move to make the bus more fashionable again. The Government has given an extra £50 million for London Bus services. One of the complaints of non-bus users is the traffic congestion, which impacts bus journeys. Bus priority lanes have helped protect buses from the worst of congestion and contributed to the reduction of journey times by some 16 per cent since 1993. Still it can be said that bus passengers get a rough deal. Less than 1 per cent of street space in London is reserved for buses, although bus passengers contribute 15 per cent of all London's road users.

Bus lanes have been introduced all over London in order to try and increase the bus speed. There will be draconian measures introduced to fine and remove non-bus traffic from the 'bus only' allocated areas. Standards on buses are set to improve dramatically with new investment in the buses themselves including low emission engines which will reduce pollution and low floor buses to allow easy access. There will also be universal air conditioning introduced. As part of the upgrade we can expect increased information available, smart card ticketing, increased interchanges with other forms of transport, a digital countdown system at bus stops and better shelter amenities. These measures are being introduced on key bus routes and will extend to the whole network by 2011.

The London congestion problem

Londoners love their independence. So much so that surveys suggest that many Londoners would rather spend up to four extra hours a day in their car rather than share their travel space with anyone else and travel by public transport! The net result of cramming thousands of individual cars through narrow 16th–18th Century streets is, of course, severe congestion. In addition the trend towards contracting out a range of non-core functions and services, and the growing demand for 'just in time' deliveries, has stimulated a boom in the number of business vehicles – for all the right reasons – on London's roads.

The cost of congestion is estimated at £5 billion to London's business community. There is a need to reduce congestion on London's roads without undue burden on London's business. The Mayor has taken a familiarly contentious position on this with the proposed introduction of congestion charging. The proposed system will be implemented by 2003.

The Mayor's congestion charging scheme will charge cars and HGVs £5 for entering an area bounded by 'the inner ring road' between the hours of 7am and 7pm. There will be exemptions for taxis, buses, emergency vehicles, alternative fuelled cars, electrically propelled vehicles, disabled passenger cars and a 90 per cent discount for residents within the zone. A weekly charge would be £25, monthly would be £110 and annual £1250. Business in principle welcomes congestion charging and the opportunity to use the price mechanism as a tool for influencing traffic flows. Intense lobbying from the business community secured a reduction in the original cost of £15 for HGV and light delivery vehicles to a rate equal with cars of £5.

The business community continues to lobby effectively on the implementation of the scheme to make sure business is minimally affected by the project.

The limit proposed for the boundary on the South and East side of the scheme is considered to extend too far into the areas where the majority of small and medium-sized enterprises, is located. 34 per cent of the SMEs[4] (1–50 employees) responding to our survey are based in East London. Most SMEs have small storage capacities dependent upon the daily deliveries from outsourcing companies. In addition, they are often operating small delivery vehicles. If the boundary were to extend into these areas, where there is a high density of SMEs, this area of the economy may suffer. Boundaries too far East of the city, would have an adverse affect on SMEs which may not be able to withstand the burden of charging, that larger business North of the river could more easily cope with.

Business largely supports the proposed hours of operation. Having said that, the effect on the restauranteur sector should be taken into account. Given the propensity for theatre and concert goers to seek an early meal before an evening event, the bar and restauranteurs consider that they will be adversely affected by later entry times. The *Halcrow Fox Road User Charging in London Report* (March 1999) suggests that 'theatreland, restaurants and cinema-goers will find that

7pm is restrictive.' With this in mind business would favour earlier cut off time for entry giving time both for private car users to reach an evening event and to enjoy bar and restaurant facilities in Central London prior to the event. Business would favour a cut off time to be 5.30pm rather than 6pm or 7pm.

Rail commuters – daily access

About 448,000 commuters use over-land train to get to work in London, accounting for some 41 per cent of the commuting traffic. So those who wish to live in a quaint English village can still do that and work in London. Again commuter railways have been undergoing major change. The rail industry was privatised five years ago having been in the public sector for some 50 years. Rail is now the fastest form of transport in the South East of England with many trains travelling over 100 miles per hour and having express services into Central London locations. Those locations are either within walking distance to the workplace or have access to underground systems. 90 per cent of the trains arrive within ten minutes of the expected arrival times.

Recently, however, there has been less than 100 per cent satisfaction with the service. Since the privatisation of the regional rail services, the track has been owned by a separate company. It is largely regarded that the track has not had the investment which it ought to have had, and recent events have required speed restrictions and huge track replacement operations. The cost to firms of the current train disruption could be up to £5 billion nationwide and £1 billion in London, according to estimates by the London Chamber of Commerce.

The disruption has resulted in lost output because of people arriving late for work and the impact that this has on morale, plus a knock-on effect in terms of cancelled business meetings, delayed deliveries and added road congestion. The disruption may also have affected Christmas shopping patterns.

There is room for optimism. Railtrack is already beating its own targets for track upgrading and replacement. Over Christmas 80 speed restrictions were eased and by the 19 January Railtrack announced that they had completed 280 miles of the 550 total requiring re-railing.

New developments

There are a number of key rail developments which will further increase access and rail over the next ten years as outlined in the ten year investment plan. Hitherto there has been a great divide between the West and the East of London. Crossrail is a £2.5 billion project which will link East London on a high speed link to West London suburbs. There will be 24 trains an hour linking the East and West networks of trains. This project will enable the large workforce in East London to benefit from the specific business developments in West London and indeed for those who choose to live in West London suburbs to be involved in much of the regeneration business which is growing in East London.

Similarly, Thameslink 2000, at a cost of £830 million, will develop a North/South link through the centre of London. This will allow 24 trains an hour to actually cross the centre of London from North to South. There will be interchanges at the strategic London underground stations and will serve to relieve much of the underground traffic.

In addition we expect to see the East London Line Extension with combined Northern and Southern line extensions, totalling a cost of £500 million, to open by 2005. An additional East London river crossing at Woolwich will facilitate greater development in East London.

Rail links to airports

London also has the largest range of rail links to airports in the world. The new Heathrow Express (a 10-minute journey) runs from Paddington Station, there are a variety of other links from Victoria, London Bridge and Waterloo to Gatwick (a new 15-minute express service is being developed), Kings Cross to Luton and Liverpool Street to Stansted.

Eurostar

One of the great luxuries of London is that it can be commutable from France or Belgium by the new Eurostar. This offers high speed services between city centres – London to Paris in three hours and London to Brussels in one hour 40 minutes. There are up to 28 trains per day.

Heliports

It is considered amongst aviation experts that London has, to date, been lacking in heliport provision to the point that it has fallen woefully short of its competitors. There is, however, a bright future for heliports in London. Harrods have set up a commercial heliport in Battersea which caters for the ever-expanding demand. Battersea heliport can handle up to 50 landings and take-offs per day. This facility is useful although many argue it is further from the City than is ideal.

Battersea heliport is the only site for helicopter activity, since the Southwark site was closed, London City Airport is specifically excluded from helicopter traffic and the Thames barge scheme quashed.

The Mayor will make no commitment to supporting calls for a comprehensive publicly-funded heliport until there is some evidence of demand, and it will largely be up to London's business community to make that demand felt.

There are a possible two types of helicopter service – the 'bus' service, carrying up to 24 chartered passengers, and the 'taxi cab' service, carrying a small number making high cost, exclusive, executive flights to a Central London destination.

Suggested sites for the London Heliport include Royal Victoria Dock and Kings Cross/St Pancras where there is a 114-acre site available. Other sites muted have been Wembley and Croydon. The Kings Cross option would afford an innovative aspect to the interchange facility of Cross Rail, CTRL extension and NE railways.

Air transport

What really puts London on the map as far as travel is concerned is its status as Europe's premier international air travel hub. London has four international airports accessed by excellent over-land routes outside London; Heathrow, Gatwick, Stansted and Luton are within 40 minutes of Central London. City Airport is within twenty minutes of the financial centre, and three smaller airports which cater for private aircraft are located within 40 minutes of the centre. In air transport terms, no other city in the world can rival London.

In 1997 airports in the London area hosted some 94 million passengers. The growth of projected passenger movement is estimated to be 155 by 2010 and 185 million by 2015. The projected growth of the demand on London airports is a three-fold increase by 2030 arriving a total figure of 290 million passenger movements – this represents an average increase in growth by 3.5 per cent per annum.

Business is pushing for the future demand for London's air services to be met because, we argue, airport development is good for business. For every 1000 people employed in an airport, there is a spin off of around 2500 jobs in the economy. Business supports the building of a fifth terminal at London's Heathrow, which will enable Heathrow's passengers to travel through the airport more quickly and efficiently therefore increasing capacity. We hope to have the Government's decision on this shortly.

Impressive meetings facilities have grown up around the main airports, with numerous hotels offering business conferences and meeting facilities. In addition, Heathrow boasts its own business centre with 20 air conditioned meeting rooms, a conference suite seating up to 60 people, theatre-style, and a business lounge. Many businesses choose to locate near the airports, capitalising on the many and various roads and rail links. The development of business parks is becoming a feature of the airport landscape.

As well as a burgeoning business market there has been dramatic growth in the availability of low cost airlines offering cheap deals of Europe's many glorious cities and indeed as a cheap and viable alternative to train travel to the UK's major cities.

In a move to create market forces to govern slot (the number of spaces available for landing and take-off) allocation, the Government wants to auction off slots at UK airports in the same way as mobile phone licenses were. The aviation industry is against this, with airlines being described as 'up in arms'. The Government has outlined in their Green Paper on Aviation that slot allocation has been made on the basis of historic precedence, so airlines holding a slot for one season will get another slot the following year on the basis that they have already held a slot. This somewhat archaic system of allocation is known as 'grandfather rights'.

Airlines are claiming that the sticky fingers of the Treasury are all over the idea of the proposed reform. Indeed the Treasury has been present at all the meetings to discuss slot allocation.

There are a number of questions to be resolved – what will happen to the domestic flight routes? In a cut and thrust market-driven system, large American airlines such as Delta will fight for position and small low cost groups may not be able to compete. This of course has implications for rural destinations and the viability of air as a mode of transport to the regions. The UK is not supported by other EU countries, who, when the UK asked for a special exception being made for the current arrangements, vocalised their opposition to the concept. The same consultants who assisted with the mobile phone auction have been appointed to work on this project.

New hope for London

London business is delighted that the Government in their White Paper – *2010: The 10 Year Plan* have pledged a total of £25 billion over ten years. This is a committed budget that will be realised when private finance initiatives are secured. So it is not a cash release as yet, but it does represent a political will to increase investment. This is something the business community has been pushing for decades.

With the growth of housing demand and vast increases in office and manufacturing spaces in London there has been a movement to traditionally poorer areas of East and South East London. Transport priorities have followed this trend which has increased the regeneration

potential of these areas. So there has been significant transport investment recently. The Mayor has inherited a £5.5 billion investment
package from the Government which includes linking East London
communities in North and South London with the light rail crossing at
Lewisham, the new state of the art Jubilee Line Extension producing
added access to South East London, the Croydon Tram link and the
M11 Link Road.

Conclusion

For the incoming business, London may seem expensive to get around
by UK standards, but in terms of the international business world,
London offers enormous opportunities in transatlantic, Asian and
European traffic. The various transport systems available are both
archaic and innovative, quaint and grand. There are frustrations, as
there are in any city, but London has a vast range of methods for getting
around and they are set to remain the best in the world.

Notes

[1] Healey and Baker is one of the world's leading commercial real estate consultants.
The survey considers the poling of 502 companies which were surveyed from nine
European countries. The sample was systematically selected from 'Europe's 15,000
largest companies'. A representative survey of industrial, trading and services companies were included. The scores shown for each city throughout the report are based
on the responses and weighted by Harris according to nominations for the best,
second best and third best.
[2] London First, CBI and London Chamber of Commerce – Transport Investment – a fair
deal for London. June 2000
[3] Performance Plan 2000. London Underground
[4] Small and Medium Sized Enterprizes

2.2

Transport: Cargo and Freight Provision

Justina Hurley, DHL

The UK is a leading trading power and financial centre, and is amongst the quartet of trillion dollar economies of Western Europe. London is one of the world's glamour capitals and is a melting pot of cultures, races and industries. There are few cities more vibrant or more intoxicating than London. According to the London Chamber of Commerce website:

- there are 567 foreign banks in London – more US banks than New York and more Japanese banks than Tokyo;
- London makes a net contribution each year of approximately £6.2 billion to the UK exchequer;
- London's economy is larger than that of Sweden, South Africa or Ireland;
- if London were a member of the EU in its own right it would constitute the sixth largest economy;
- it is estimated that consumption in London directly supports over four million jobs in the UK.

Excellent business location

All of this of course conspires to make London one of the best business locations in the world. Surrounded by five airports, and with direct road and rail connections to the rest of the UK and Europe, there are very few destinations in the world more than a three day express delivery distance from London – while most of the key business destinations are just a delivery day away if using an air express service.

For bulk exports and heavy freight, less reliant on time pressure, London is well serviced by haulier and sea freight companies. Continental Europe is mainly serviced by short and long haul trucking companies, the main exit ports being Portsmouth, Dover, and, via the Channel Tunnel, at Folkstone. Long distance overseas routes to destinations such as Australasia and the Americas can choose from a range of air and sea freight options.

However, most businesses in London rely on speed. It's a buzzed-up city and perhaps second only to New York in its 'want it yesterday' attitude. The main London businesses break into four main sectors: financial & legal, media, print and publishing and fashion/textiles. Most smaller businesses feed off from or support these main sectors in some way or another. Outer London is home to a wider variety of businesses, from hi-tech, automotive and telecoms to pharmaceutical, engineering and computing.

Moving the goods

Within London there is a veritable gamut of city-based couriers who specialise in deliveries between businesses. There is also a wide selection of same day and next day domestic couriers who specialise in moving goods within the UK only. The Yellow Pages or word of mouth referrals are the best means of finding a good city or domestic carrier.

The need for speed

The next rung of the ladder is the international air express offering. The top four global operators – DHL, FedEx, UPS and TNT – all have a UK operation. As an indication of the market size, DHL, which has a 50 per cent market share in the UK, moves, on average, over two and a half thousand tonnes per week and deals with over 22 million shipments per year as part of its UK operation. Using Heathrow, Luton and East Midlands airports to serve its London customer base, DHL also has 11 depots in the London area to facilitate customer needs. In addition, it has branched out to offer express logistics and express distribution services to businesses that require spare parts management, warehousing or after-sales care services, but who don't want to have to source the infrastructure or to directly manage the supply chain themselves.

Clean delivery

Like any city, traffic in London is busy and there are restricted zones, open to public transport and taxis only, so delivery solutions have to be innovative. DHL for example, in an effort to be environmentally respon-sible as well as efficient, uses a team of walking couriers and couriers riding eco-efficiency quadricycles, plus a fleet of electric cars and LPG vans in the busy inner city areas.

Greater London

The outskirts of London are equally busy and as well serviced as Central London. The M4 corridor, with its proximity to Heathrow, is dotted with the names of probably every famous corporation, hotel group and cargo company that one can think of.

Circling the Greater London area is the infamous M25 which, in transportation terms, is not as bad as it is painted and, when chanced upon at off-peak times, is an excellent connecting route between London and the various airports that service the transportation industry. At DHL, for example, we use Heathrow, Luton and East Midlands to move goods to and from London. The route chosen will depend on the time of collection and the speed of delivery required. For example, a shipment bound for a next-day delivery to, say, Paris, could follow one of two routes. Depending on the time that it is collected and the space availability on the various aircraft, it could go either from the DHL sorting hub at London Heathrow or from the DHL East Midlands Hub. From either location it will go on to the DHL Brussels sorting hub from where it is then routed to Paris. In either case it will arrive at its destina-tion in Paris the next morning ready for delivery. This is just an example, as the routing will obviously vary according to the destination country.

Understanding the delivery challenges

In reality it's all very well to know what modes of transportation are available to London-based businesses – in short, you name it and London can provide it. In this era of supply chain and time critical deliveries however, the more pertinent question is 'are London busi-nesses using these distribution options effectively within a strategic exporting framework?' And, in addition, 'are companies really thinking about the untapped export or import opportunities they may be missing?'

As far back as 1998 the OECD noted that 'the volume of world merchandise trade is 16 times greater today than it was in 1950, as compared to a six-fold increase in the volume of world production.' UK trade figures have shown consistent growth in recent years. However, our share of this rapidly growing global market is actually diminishing. With a third of UK GDP and UK jobs reliant on international trade, effective and successful exporting is of core importance to all sectors of the UK economy.

Over 100,000 small to medium-sized companies currently export. There are clearly many more that could expand and enhance their profitability, by targeting new overseas markets. 'The challenge', according to Ian Campbell, Director General, Institute of Export, 'is to raise awareness of the opportunities presented by exporting and to remove the 'fear factor' from international trade.'

Every quarter DHL polls 1000 exporters in the UK to track levels of exporting confidence, key markets and general exporting trends. This survey, called the DHL Quarterly Export Indicator (QEI), shows that more than a third of exporters in the London area are committing resource both to promote goods abroad and to invest in new product development. Though exchange rates definitely have an impact on UK business, key export destinations are currently the EU, Western Europe and the USA, with the Middle East, South East Asia and Eastern Europe also proving popular. China in particular is becoming an increasingly popular export destination.

The rise of the Internet has created an affordable shop window through which small to medium-sized enterprises can advertise their wares to a global community. But it is not as simple as just designing a good website, choosing a distribution company and then sitting back to let it unfold. Rather, internet culture has created a sense of immediacy in all aspects of business and therefore delivery of export support must aim to be seamless – internationally, nationally and regionally. The DHL world-wide network amongst others, is often the gateway through which many small businesses are able to reach the rest of the world.

Internet technology isn't just about e-commerce. Information systems are also faster, more visible and globally harmonised. Therefore, design, specification, delivery and prices can be compared internationally in minutes. Orders can be switched away from traditional suppliers overnight. The goal of effective supply chain management therefore is to build relationships that encourage suppliers and customers to work together to resolve problems and develop enhanced solutions rather than dissolve partnerships needlessly. The goal is also to interface a company's marketplace, distribution network, production process and procurement activities so as to enable exporters to provide higher levels of service to customers whilst reducing their own costs.

Supply chain management

According to Alan Waller of PricewaterhouseCoopers 'Nowadays, it's supply chains that compete with supply chains, not companies with companies.' The 'Supply Chain' is a sequence of events intended to satisfy a customer's demand for goods. It consists of purchasing, production, warehousing, inventory management and distribution.

International emphasis is increasingly on customer service. Factors such as time critical delivery requirements and globalisation mean that organisational integration and careful selection of distribution partners can be the key to gaining competitive advantage in the marketplace. The challenge is to deliver added value and service excellence, consistently, at every stage in the supply chain. Just-in-time delivery, outsourcing, global sourcing potential, and diversified transport options mean that customers have more choice than ever before.

The key is partnership

Increasingly, customers want not only just-in-time deliveries, but also variable quantities and urgent exception orders. Shorter product life cycles are reducing the time in which profits can be made. Traditionally, marketing, distribution, planning, manufacturing and purchasing organisations have operated independently, each with their own objectives. Today effective supply chain management is fast becoming a corporate priority – companies need to integrate their suppliers' suppliers with their customers' customers.

Success in exporting or importing is as much about the choice of transportation and distribution partner as it is about the way the goods are sold. London-based businesses are very fortunate as they have a wide range of distribution partners from which to choose. A good working relationship with the chosen carrier is vital as the carrier should be able to offer a lot more than just a 'delivery service.' DHL, for example has a 'consultancy' approach whereby sales staff review customer needs first and help the customer choose a best practice delivery solution. In addition, support staff can advise on the most efficient ways of navigating the complicated – but mandatory – export and import paperwork and explain the regulations governing these requirements not just for the UK, but for any destination world-wide.

Required paperwork

Every shipment, whether international or domestic, requires an air waybill. An air waybill is a consignment note that details all the information necessary for sending a package e.g. who it is from, where it is going, whether it is a document or a parcel, and finally its weight, size and value. In addition to the air waybill, a customs invoice is required when sending dutiable goods to countries other than the EU.

Invoices must be originals and have to be completed on company letterheads. The invoices must be typewritten and should not have any hand-written or obvious typewritten corrections. Details given on the invoice must match those given on the air waybill. The language on the invoice should be English and a minimum of three original invoices is required. In all cases, failure to complete the invoice correctly can result in the return of goods to the UK or in the seizure of the goods by customs until the correct paperwork is produced.

Types of invoice

Proforma Invoice

For use when sending goods for which no charge is being made (i.e. goods that are not for resale).

Commercial Invoice

For use when the goods are part of a commercial transaction (goods being sold).

Duty & VAT

All goods imported into the UK from outside the EC must be declared to HM Customs & Excise and, in most cases, are subject to Customs Duty and VAT. This includes goods bought over the Internet.

Customs Duty is a tax levied on goods produced outside the EU. In broad terms, it is designed to bring the cost of these goods up to the same level as those produced within the EU. Once duty is paid, the goods are in 'free circulation' and can move throughout the EU without restriction.

The rate of duty for any given product being imported into the EU may differ depending upon the country of origin. Set annually by the EU, rates run from 1 January to 31 December and are published in a Customs Tariff issued by each EU country. Duty is usually percentage-based, and averages between 5–9 per cent with extremes of 0 and 85 per cent.

Goods are classified by customs code in order to arrive at the rate of Duty. The EU uses a ten digit coding and there are approximately 14,000 classifications. The value on which duty is based is normally the cost of the goods, plus the cost of transporting them to the EU border.

Another type of duty, known as Excise Duty, covers certain goods such as; wines, spirits, cigars, cigarettes and tobacco. When you buy goods in the UK, the price you pay includes this tax. However if you import these goods either from the EU or from outside the EU, you will have to pay excise duty and VAT on top.

VAT is a tax normally levied on the supply of goods (and services) made by a VAT registered business. However, imported goods are also subject to VAT. This is to prevent a purchaser gaining an unfair advantage by buying non-EU goods VAT free. Most goods are subject to VAT at the current standard rate of 17.5 per cent. However, some goods including books and certain other publications together with children's clothing, are not subject to VAT ('Zero-rated'). The value on which VAT is based is normally the cost of the goods, plus the cost of transporting them to the consignee's address in the UK. However, we must add to this the amount of Customs Duty paid before calculating VAT. The consignee is legally obliged to pay Duty and VAT except where the consignor has agreed to accept these charges in the contract of sale.

How are the charges paid?

Goods cannot be delivered until HM Customs has received all duty and VAT charges owed. Express carriers, such as DHL, will have an account with HM Customs, known as a deferment account, and will pay the duty and VAT charges on the shipper's behalf, invoicing the shipper for this service separately after delivery. Some businesses have their own deferment accounts with HM Customs and Excise and in those cases the express carrier will merely arrange for their customer's account to be directly debited by Customs.

An administration fee is normally charged for inbound goods incurring duty and VAT charges. The amount charged is 2 per cent of the total duty and VAT costs with a minimum fee of £10.00 for business accounts and, in DHL's case, in recognition of the growth of e-commerce the minimum administration fee for private individuals has been set at £1.25.

If you are VAT registered you may be able to recover the VAT. But duty and administration charges are not recoverable.

You can find more information on Duty and VAT by visiting the Customs website at www.hmce.gov.uk or by contacting your local customs office.

Shopping on the net

The import/export market has traditionally been a business to business arena with all parties very fluent in duty and VAT requirements, licence applications where relevant and general administrative procedures.

One of the biggest problems DHL has found with the growth of e-shopping is that the net shopper very often does not understand what purchasing on the net actually means. In effect, as soon as they hit the return key to purchase a product from a non UK origin, then e-purchasers effectively become importers and are subject to any applicable duty and VAT payments – as highlighted earlier.

Internet sites are not obliged to shout about this information and very often it will be found in the small print, if at all. The customer buys from a company, the shipment is delivered and then after this an invoice for duty and VAT will arrive. The customer is often taken by surprise and doesn't always realise that, unless the supplier has contractually agreed to pay duty and VAT (and this is very rarely the case), the liability for payment falls to the importer. It is wise to consider though that a customer caught unawares rarely wants to repeat the experience, while a customer who feels that you have done as much as you can to hand hold them through the Internet buying decision process is likely to return to your site.

Therefore, businesses that may be thinking of setting up e-commerce portals should be aware of what it entails and should do as much as they can to explain the process to potential customers. Again, DHL always advises that you talk to your delivery partner as companies such as DHL have the expertise to help you to provide your customers with the best information.

What Air Express can offer you – mainstream services

Standard Air Express

This is the express international door-to-door delivery of documents, and dutiable and non-dutiable goods. Prices for this type of service typically start at around £18 for the first half-kilo, and rises in half-kilo increments. This price range assumes a mid-sized shipper.

Import services

A service which allows the importer to set up and manage an account in the UK, pay in sterling and yet transactions all originate in the countries outside of the UK.

Mail

If your business sends mail overseas, either regularly or in large (quantities of 1000 and above) one-off quantities, then always look at mail products and shop around for quotes before you go with what seems like the most obvious solution.

Non-standard shipments

Items which are exceptionally heavy, large or just unusual, can usually be managed by an air express company, but may not be advertised as standard offerings. DHL, for example, has an agent operated road and sea freight service that can be offered to all DHL UK account holders. The services offered are dependent on the destination. Whether door to depot or door to port, again the delivery method is dependent on the service required and the destination country. However you should always talk through what you need with your provider as there is usually a solution that will suit.

Express Logistics

The small to medium enterprise can trade on a global basis if a smart approach is taken to cargo and freight provision. Logistics is no longer an exclusive club that only the bulk operator can join. DHL, for example, has coined the phrase 'Express Logistics' to speak about a whole new way of doing business internationally. In the DHL definition, Express Logistics is the outsourcing of warehousing, inventory and information management and transportation using express distribution to create a completely integrated solution. As Cranfield University's 'logistics guru' Professor Martin Christopher comments, 'The prizes in today's markets go only to those companies that are capable of providing added value in ever-shortening time scales.'

Choice of solution

The solutions listed below are just examples of the express logistics and express distribution solutions that DHL offers to customers. They are included, not to give a detailed explanation of how it all works, but to demonstrate that no business should feel that it is limited by its size. Storage space, distance or after sales care problems can all become part of a solution if the right distribution partner is chosen.

Express Logistics/Express Distribution

Usually there are specialised export and import solutions for various types of product. The range includes:

Strategic inventory management

This is the complete control of physical and information process flows involved in managing a time-critical service contract. DHL currently has 100 Spare Parts Centres (SPCs) strategically located around Europe. The network of SPCs can all be interlinked by using DHL's in-house network systems. These systems provide the necessary control of receipt, storage and dispatch of spares. Each item is given a part number which records stock quantity and location in the SPC. Key benefits are:

- reliable, high speed delivery (2–4 hours) of spare parts;
- 24 hours a day, 7 days a week regional, European and even global coverage;
- a single partner, one-stop shop;
- simplified and centralised information and communication;
- storage of spares at strategic locations;
- effective and efficient returns of parts;
- business information systems that give overall visibility and control.

Direct express inventory

This is the management of centralised inventory, related information and express distribution of goods and/or component parts within a promised time window. The primary goal of Direct Express Inventory is to provide UK businesses with the opportunity to expand into new markets at lower costs with reduced risks. What this means in reality is that the customer can use DHL facilities to centralise and manage inventory regionally. Direct Express Inventory is particularly useful for low cost and low risk entry into new and emerging markets across the world. Key benefits are:

- improved service levels – fast delivery;
- increased efficiency and transparency in the logistics pipeline – at a lower cost;
- allows concentration on core activities – outsourcing distribution;
- effective and efficient way of trading internationally in terms of service levels, costs and access to DHL expertise on the varied export regulations which govern individual countries.

Return repair inventory

This is the management of a complete pick-up and delivery cycle by DHL. This includes the packaging and documentation required to move defective, repaired and replacement parts between the customer and a DHL Express Logistics and Repair Centre. This involves managing the inventory and shipment information throughout the whole process – liaising with both shippers and receivers on line. Key benefits are:

* improved 'after sales' customer care;
* increased efficiency and transparency in the logistics pipeline;
* reduced overall operating costs;
* allows concentration on core activities;
* effective and efficient returns of parts;
* central repair instead of local third-party vendors creates greater control of repairs.

Repair exchange

This is the management of the physical movement of failed equipment and components or replacements, between the point of use and the customer's own repair facility. Key benefits are:

* increased customer satisfaction via reduced downtime;
* economies of scale from centralised repair facilities;
* more control over shipments and the exchange process;
* detailed reporting on exceptions and performance;
* lower inventory costs;
* focus on sales – no service 'headaches';
* no specialist technical knowledge required;
* reduced time/money invested in service;
* unique and powerful sales tool – it is convenient, easy, fast and it works.

Finished goods

This involves the movement of a product from a manufacturer or distributor direct to the end customer or consumer as fast as possible without being delayed in a warehouse at any point. Key benefits are:

* customer orders are delivered faster;
* quicker invoicing enables quicker cash collection;
* better control over quality and delivery performance standards with centralised production and configuration;
* local stock is no longer necessary or is reduced substantially, along with the costs of manufacturing and storing the stock;
* risk of stock obsolescence is reduced;
* shorter lines between manufacturer and customer enables efficient and responsive product upgrades in changing market requirements.

Spare parts

This involves the express delivery of spare parts direct from customers' inventory locations to their field service users for the repair of critical equipment. Key benefits are:

- greater control over costs and performance standards by consolidating and rationalising operations;
- more productive field service engineers;
- reduced inventory holding costs;
- stock duplication eliminated via one central store;
- improved flexibility in collection and delivery times;
- access to an extended network of drop-off points based on the geographic distribution of customers;
- less reliance on local third party suppliers.

Planned production support

This is the 'Just-In-Time' delivery of raw materials to support a manufacturing process requiring minimal inventory. Key benefits are:

- shorter lead times and quicker procurement;
- less stock means more flexibility to upgrade or redesign products;
- reduced capital tied up in stock and warehousing means that cash can be used more productively elsewhere.

Goods samples

These are tailored distribution solutions involving the express delivery of product samples for ordering or final production approval. Key benefits are:

- quicker product launches;
- security of new designs;
- reduced ordering cycle times;
- more efficient sales processes;
- enhanced buyer relations.

Financial services

This is the express delivery of time-critical financial instruments for correspondent banks. Key benefits are:

- maximised earnings with priority service for 'Cash Letter/Letters of Credit';
- increased productivity ;
- more efficient processes which increase earnings while reducing costs;
- improved customer service levels and customer loyalty;
- higher security on valuables

Test services

Express delivery of specimens and supplies, for their immediate use or return for testing. When used in combination with the DHL Worldwide Express Network, the medical service – called Worldwide Medical Express – provides clients with an effective integrated service to move medicines, vaccines, diagnostic specimens and clinical trial supplies to market. Key benefits are:

- ability to standardise processes for international tests and product distribution;
- improved uniformity in testing results through a single laboratory;
- reduced development time means quicker time to market for new products;
- reductions in the high costs of lost specimens and supplies;
- increased profits and a competitive advantage from better distribution management.

How to get the most from your distribution partner

The most important part is to know where to start. If you don't really know what you are looking for, then it is unlikely that the customer service call centre personnel will be able to help you there and then. They are usually specially trained to take bookings and to refer inquiries to the appropriate teams.

It is best to tell them immediately that you have a business inquiry, but don't know what type of account will suit you best and so you are in need of advice. They will then arrange for a sales person to call you back. Alternatively, most air express companies have Service Centres (DHL, for example, has 53 in the UK). These are offices that operate as drop-off locations and as local sales and support offices. It is always worth asking if there is a Service Centre in your area and if so to request the sales manager to contact you.

For more specialised accounts needing bespoke solutions, there are special consultants who will help you develop the solution which best suits your business requirements. Again you will be directed to these personnel once an initial sales contact has assessed what you are looking for.

The most important advice we can give is to be fully open about what you expect and what you are looking for. Put the time in at the beginning to really work with your air express partner to get the process up and running and work with them to iron out any hitches. Be wary of companies that tell you anything is possible – it isn't! But there are usually other options that they can suggest as alternatives. If you are advertising abroad or trading on the Internet, tell your distribution partner what you are offering. Support staff are used to dealing with these destinations and will usually be able to advise on any issues that may arise if you are unfamiliar with the regulations in these countries. More than anything else be realistic about what you can and cannot achieve. The better your understanding of the exporting process, the better the relationship you will have with all your export contacts.

Further information:

www.dhlmasterclass.com – a website that is intended to act as a source of business intelligence for SMEs and help guide them in their transition from traditional non-internet business into e-business.

www.dhl.co.uk – this website has a section on exporting that covers many of the issues surrounding exporting. Full information is available also on required forms, air waybills, how to track packages etc.

Part 3

The Central London Office Market

you can't over emphasise it's importance

WWW. **ADAMS•BURNETT** .COM

Corporate Property Advisers

your link to the London Commercial Property Market

Adams Burnett is an independent, dynamic firm of corporate property advisers providing a comprehensive service on property strategy, the acquisition and disposal of property and associated professional services aimed at commercial occupiers.

We listen to our clients, seek to understand their property problems and use our skill and experience to achieve client objectives through an agreed strategy.

Acquired 51,300 sq.ft in London on behalf of Marathon Oil

Adams Burnett is built on offering a bespoke service. We recognise every instruction is unique and tailor our approach to the needs of your business requirements.

Step by step personal involvement by the Partners, John Adams, Paul Burnett and Eddie Robinson, ensures that your business objective is at the forefront of our commitment. All instructions receive the same high standard of professional service and expertise.

We are a dedicated, pro-active and focused team. Our aim is to ensure clients receive advice which is independent, forward thinking, innovative and most importantly, effective. Your relationship with us is based upon trust and integrity.

Our experience confirms that strategic planning, close monitoring of the clients' specific needs and a structured approach to tasks will always ensure the best results.

Our international client base covers a wide range of industry sectors including oil, computer hardware, computer software, manufacturing, financial, insurance, recruitment, media, management consultants and solicitors.

Acquired 50,000 sq.ft at Savoy Court, London on behalf of Booz Allen & Hamilton

ADAMS•BURNETT

2 Caxton Street
London SW1H 0QE
Tel: 020 7233 0200
Fax: 020 7233 0500
email: info@adamsburnett.com
www.adamsburnett.com

Acquired 18,750 sq.ft in Berkeley Square House, London on behalf of Arthur D Little

It's all down to experience...

ATIS REAL Weatheralls

REAL PEOPLE
REAL SOLUTIONS
REAL ESTATE

Our London offices:

Jonathan Morton (jonathan.morton@atisweatheralls.com)
22 Chancery Lane, London WC2A 1LT
T: 020 7338 4000   F: 020 7430 2628

Greg Cooke (greg.cooke@atisweatheralls.com)
Norfolk House, 31 St James's Square, London SW1Y 4JR
T: 020 7338 4200   F: 020 7493 0746

Donald Mark (donald.mark@atisweatheralls.com)
Level 16 City Tower, 40 Basinghall Street, London EC2V 5DE
T: 020 7338 4400   F: 020 588 4542

For further details visit: www.atisweatheralls.com

We are part of one of Europe's largest property consultancies, the ATIS REAL Group, employing over 2000 staff and fee earners in 62 offices across Europe. We are the number one company in France and Germany, through ATIS REAL Auguste-Thouard and ATIS REAL Müller International.

With associated offices throughout the USA, Far East, Scandinavia and Central and Eastern Europe, we offer our clients a truly international service.

At ATIS REAL Weatheralls, we deliver quality strategic and commercial solutions to occupiers and investors, providing a full range of property services which are effective, client focused and based on our market knowledge and experience.

Our values are integrity, excellence and professionalism combined with energy and innovation.

We measure our performance by client satisfaction, market recognition and financial success, and by our ability to attract and motivate the highest calibre of people.

We boast a broad blue-chip client portfolio, which includes:

- Microsoft
- IBM
- Hewlett Packard
- Merrill Lynch Europe
- PricewaterhouseCoopers
- Nomura International
- Andersens
- Yahoo

Whether your outlook is UK or international focused, ATIS REAL Weatheralls has the remedy for your property headaches.

we make things happen

we do
rated Support Services
Property Management
Property Services
Property Legislation

We're providing Integrated Facilities Management
to businesses across London and beyond. Our customer-
focused solutions are raising quality and service levels
in spaces as diverse as Butlins holiday centres and the
Chelsea and Westminster hospital.

Our wide range of non-core property and
support services includes building control approval,
extensions and refurbishments, car park
management, reception, cleaning and security.
Altogether we look after 100 million sq ft of
property, so if anyone has the capability to
deliver long-term, strategic Integrated Facilities
Management, we do.

carillion

For information, contact Graham Blow, Operations Director, **Carillion Services**
T+44(0)20 8380 5233 F+44(0)20 8380 5060 www.carillionplc.com

Carillion Services Limited
Westlink House, 981 Great West Road,
Brentford, Middlesex TW8 9DN

Contact: Graham Blow, Operations Director
Tel: +44 (0)208 3805233 Fax: +44 (0) 208 3805060
e-mail: blow.graham@carillionplc.com Internet: www.carillionplc.com

Parent Company:	Carillion PLC
Managing Director:	Gordon Bryden
Number of Employees:	c.2400
Turnover	£166m
Pre-Tax Profit	£4.0m
Year End	December

COMPANY PROFILE

Delivering integrated facilities management solutions to exceed expectations of building performance and service levels by creating and sustaining a quality business support environment, is Carillion Services core business.

We offer a unique development of approaches to service delivery that directly reflects the current and future needs of organisations, and in so doing, challenges the traditional service support industry.

With parent strength of c.£1.9bn, ability to manage risk on major projects, PFI/PPP schemes and a blue chip client portfolio, Carillion Services are able to deliver focused solutions to meet clients' facilities and property-related needs in an ever-changing commercial and operational environment.

By focusing on developing strategic partnerships and acting as both catalyst and manager of change within our client organisations, the strength of our service is our ability to prioritise functions and integrate business management re-engineering with proven property management methods against customer's business objectives. The result is better value for the customer and improved quality for the end user.

We provide integrated facilities management to over 100 million square feet of public and private property throughout the UK, including the estates of the MOD and the Metropolitan Police Service. We are the leading providers of non-clinical support services to the NHS, with substantial PFI expertise. We also provide insurance brooking and risk related management with Markfield Insurance. Our services also include the provision of fully integrated and modular fleet management services within an environment which both serves to deliver excellence to the customer and optimises the commercial performance of the business.

We are continuously developing our services within the UK and on an International scope. With our parent company, we have that support from our international division with offices located in Canada, France, The Caribbean, Republic of Ireland, Oman, United Arab Emirates and Germany.

Selection of Clients

- BT Project Jaguar - Montray   • London Underground Limited
- Metropolitan Police Service   • Ministry of Defence/Defence Works Services
- Railtrack plc   • Royal Parks Agency
- Chelsea & Westminster Healthcare NHS trust and Chelsea & Westminster hospital
- Essex Rivers Healthcare NHS Trust and Colchester General hospital
- Westminster City Council

3.1

The Central London Office Market in 2001

Catherine Jones,
Property Market Analyst, King Sturge

The core of the Central London Office Market is presently constrained by its own scarcity of space. It has boomed in 2000 but it is unlikely that it will slump; instead, because of the scarcity of space, rents will continue to grow, but at a more sustainable level in 2001.

Setting the scene

Defining the Central London Office Market has become increasingly more difficult with time. Traditionally the core comprised the fashionable West End and the financial centre of the City. In addition, a further (historically less popular) market, Mid Town, linked these two core markets together.

More recently the continuing popularity of these three key office markets has forced occupiers to look further afield; the result is a number of newly emerging fringe locations. The impact on the Central London Office Market as a whole has been significant, it has become less defined as its boundaries are blurred with the absorption of areas such as Docklands and Paddington. Further, the inter-relation between the core and the fringe has given rise to a number of issues that inevitably will shape the future of the Capital's office market structure.

Much of the success of Central London as an office market is due to the high level of demand for office space from a variety of international companies. Its popularity cannot be traced to any one feature, but that the core especially, satisfies many requirements for all types of occupier.

The City is a global financial centre and often the first choice as an international business location. A bank, for example, benefits from proximity to other financial institutions and associated professions such as accountants and lawyers. London's time zone also allows business to retain a key trading position in global markets, in terms of timing, while English remains the primary international business language.

The West End benefits from its postcodes and sub-markets where certain addresses, especially those in St James's and Mayfair, are traditionally favoured to create the right 'corporate image'. In recent years, other contemporary image concerns, especially in the media industry, have contributed to the popularity of trendy areas like Soho.

The year 2000 was a dramatic year for the Central London Core Office Market characterised by high demand, falling supply and record-breaking rents. The tables below highlight these trends.

Within the West End, demand was driven by a buoyant economy and the emerging technology, media and telecommunications (TMT) sector hungrily acquiring space. This, together with cautious development activity, contributed to falling availability. West End headline rents were

Table 3.1.1: *End-Year 2000 – Headline Rents in Central London*

Market	Per m² p.a.	Per ft² p.m.
City	£646	£60
West End	£926	£86
Docklands	£452	£42
Paddington	£377	£35

Source: King Sturge Research

Table 3.1.2: *Core London Office Market – Availability*

000m²	End – 1999	End – 2000	% Change
City	547.120	179.950	−67
West End	213.253	159.328	−25

Source: King Sturge Research

Table 3.1.3: *Core London Office Market – Take-Up*

000m²	1999	2000	% Change
City	381.620	657.330	72
West End	228.370	379.037	66

Source: King Sturge Research

indicative of these changes, especially the tight supply, and consequently rose to levels as high as £926/m² (£86/ft²) last achieved in the previous boom. However in real terms, rents have not yet reached the heights of the 1980s, the effect of inflation alone pushes the West End 1989 rental level up to £1091/m² (£107/ft²) at the end of 2000.

The City also saw a boost in demand with large requirements from the financial sector. There was also strong demand from non-financial Internet companies and lawyers, who helped to widen the traditionally narrow tenant base of the City. Similar trends in development activity, such as those seen in the West End, also meant that the City saw a diminishing supply of available stock and a rise in headline rents to £646/m² (£60/ft²).

It is also important to note that the Central London Office Market was the first in Europe to recover from the 1993 recession and that the current office 'boom' has lasted longer than all previous 'booms'. A contributory factor to the previous property slump was the excessive amount of speculative development that preceded it in 1988/89. The longevity of the current boom may therefore be attributed to less speculative development activity this time round and developer's preference for pre-let schemes.

Role of the fringe

With large development schemes taking form at Paddington Basin to the West, London Bridge to the South and Canary Wharf to the East, the fringe became increasingly more important throughout 2000.

The supply constraints and rocketing rents in the core forced many occupiers to look to the fringe areas for available space. These markets are not only cheaper than the core, but they also have large-sized floor plates which are currently not available anywhere else in Central London. In response to this increasing demand, the fringe, traditionally overshadowed by the West End and the City, has also benefited from rising rental levels.

The success of areas such as Docklands and Paddington will only become apparent with time. As they stand, they could be described as business parks within Central London. Paddington has direct links to Heathrow, and Docklands is well connected with the DLR and the recently completed Jubilee Line. Both are mixed use schemes, with amenities and services as part of the package. A potential problem of the future is whether these sites remain isolated from the area they are built within or whether knock-on development (which is obviously preferable) will occur.

Looking to the future

The Central London office market in 2001 is expected to be less volatile, while remaining buoyant. Recent research suggests a slow-down in growth rates within the property market as a whole: The Central London Office market is expected to respond to this. Market activity will cool, but still continue to out-perform the property market as a whole.

Within the West End, take-up will continue but at a slower rate in response to reduced supply. Subsequently, rental levels will continue to rise but at a slower and more sustainable rate. Additionally, troubles in the TMT sector and occupier migration to fringe areas will help to free up space and ease demand. The development pipeline will continue to provide much-needed new space but without the overhang of supply seen in the 1980s boom.

It is widely perceived that the City market lags just behind the West End and with a consistent level of strong demand and take-up, rents will continue to rise to further record-breaking levels (though not quite as high as the West End) and supply will be squeezed even tighter.

The role of the fringe will become more defined as the markets establish themselves. Undoubtedly, as Paddington and Docklands are completed there will be further outward movement as the West End moves West and the City moves East. Continued integration of these schemes into both their localities and the Central London Office Market as a whole will determine their success.

Let the record speak for itself

BWA Facilities Consultancy
Benchmarking costs and performance
Bank of England
Kodak
BP
British Steel
British Airways
National Air Traffic Services
Chase Manhattan Bank
Department of Trade & Industry
Bank of America
British Council
Oxford University Press
One 2 One
Powergen
Royal Mail
Zurich Financial Services
Shell UK/Italia/International
Department of Education & Employment
WH Smith

BWA Facilities Consultancy
Management Consultancy
Orange
Royal Bank of Scotland
British American Tobacco
Kodak
Kent County Council
Herts county Council
Department of Trade & Industry
Oxford University Press
British Aerospace
MAFF
Salomon Smith Barney
Post Office Counters
Lloyds TSB
Chichester College of H.E.
Bath College of H.E.
Superdrug
British Airways
Home Office Probation Service
Direct Line Insurance

PFI Projects
MoD Whitehall
STEPS
Home Office - HQ
The Treasury - HQ
DSS Longbenton
New Law Hospital
Kings College Medical School
Dartford and Gravesham Hospital
Glasgow/Haringey Schools
Stafford Two Schools
GCHQ
Colchester Barracks
Chelsea Barracks
Middlesex Hospital
St Davids Community Hospital

BWA Project Services
Project management and cost control
St. Martin's Property
Salomon Smith Barney
Department of Trade & Industry
Financial Services Authority
Financial Services Ombudsman
GAP Stores
Midland Bank (HSBC)
Bradfield College
DG Bank
McKinsey & Co
Eversheds
PPP Columbia Healthcare
Building Research Establishment

BWA Programs
Frisqué - Facilities Risk and Quality Evaluation Program
FacPOL - Model Facilities Policy Program
PremCON - Condition Scoring System
PremFINANCE- Facilities Budget Control System
FacQUAL - User Satisfaction Surveys
BQA - Building Quality Assessment
BWA Life-Cycle Costing Models

BWA
BERNARD WILLIAMS ASSOCIATES
CHARTERED SURVEYORS · BUILDING ECONOMISTS

...to name but a few!

KINGS HOUSE, 32-40 WIDMORE ROAD, BROMLEY, KENT BR1 1RY
Telephone: 020 8160 1111 Fax: 020 8161 1167
E-mail: bwa@bwassoc.co.uk Website: bwassoc.co.uk
Also at Leeds and Frankfurt

London – a centre for world-class facilities management

Bernard Williams FRICS – principal author of 'Facilities Economics in the EU' explains the importance of facilities management to overall business efficiency and how London is leading the way in the application of state-of-the art facilities management practice

Introduction

'Facilities' is a modern-day management term embracing all the accommodation and services needed to support an organisation's core activities. So, an office building is a facility but so are the photocopiers, the mailroom, the staff restaurant, the computers, the fitness centre and all the other services within it.

A broadly drawn scope of what facilities management is all about is given at Fig. A.

Fig A – *Broadly drawn scope of FM*

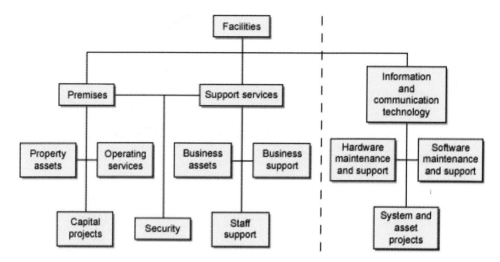

A fast-developing profession

Facilities management is defined in 'Facilities Economics' as 'the process by which the premises and support services required to support core business activities are identified, specified, procured and delivered'. Like a lot of our latter-day best practice management theory the need for this to be a separate discipline was first identified and applied in the USA. Their International Facilities Management Association (IFMA), formed in 1980, now has 20,000 or so members with representation from some 67 countries, including its UK chapter.

However, the UK was quick to latch on to the concept that facilities management could be a dynamic productivity driver in its own right; so, as early as 1991 The Centre for Facilities Management was set up at the University of Strathclyde (now moved to the University of Salford) and in no time at all was producing Masters graduates and the occasional Ph.D in Facilities Management.

2 years later the British Institute of Facilities Management was formed; it now has over 6,000 members, all of whom subscribe to a professional Code of Conduct and its own examined professional qualification BIFM (Qual). Add to this the fact that the UK now boasts getting on for 30 higher education courses – from HND to Masters Degree – in Facilities Management and it becomes clear that the UK has not only taken up this new discipline but run with it – with a vengeance!

Increasing cost and value

A major factor in catapulting the fm discipline into the forefront of business activity has been the rapid changes in ways of working. The office building of 2001 may still bear some external resemblance to its 1981 counterpart but that is where the similarities end. As someone put it 'the old house has got a new engine in it'; that engine is far more sophisticated than the old one, costs a lot more to provide and maintain and gets closer and closer to the core business activity in terms of the latter's operational effectiveness.

The cost of provision is greater, the return on the investment even more so. Therefore, de facto, the process of managing it gets more and more important with every e-mail going in and out of the system, every cubic metre of conditioned air pumped into the workspace, every roast potato joining the gammon and egg on the plate, every letter popped into the in-tray: the list of potential service categories from which to draw such reference points is about 30.

The list of cost centres currently available on the Frisqué (Facilities Risk and Quality Evaluation) benchmarking program (see Fig. B.) is comprehensive but not exhaustive.

Fig. B – *Extract from Frisqué benchmarking program showing cost centres available and selected (ticked)*

Category	Select
Services maintenance a	☐
Fabric maintenance and	☑
Grounds maintenance a	☑
Furniture maintenance a	☐
Equipment maintenance	☐
Alterations and fitting ou	☐
Cleaning	☑
Laundry	☐
Security & reception	☑
Utilities	☑
Internal decor	☐
Archiving	☑
Reprographics	☑
Stationery	☑
IT Communications	☐
IT Computers	☐
Distribution	☑
Text preparation	☐
Transport / fleet manag	☐
Catering	☑
Porterage	☑
Helpdesk / MIS	☑
Travel	☐
General management	☒
Professional services	☐
Fitness centre	☐
Nursery / creche	☐
Occupational health ser	☐

London – a magnet for top facilities managers

All UK's major commercial centres flaunt the kind of buildings alluded to above (many of which qualify to be described as 'intelligent buildings') and the same goes for most of their competitors in Europe and beyond. Nevertheless, London is showing the rest of Europe the way when it comes to 'intelligent buildings' with, for example, the magnificent dockside development at Canary Wharf setting new reference points for quality of design, construction and infrastructure. Not surprising, therefore, that the UK's new and burgeoning breed of highly educated facilities managers have been drawn to the capital as if by a magnet. Once there, their driving ambition is to make their facilities the best around.

And they do, and here is how . . .

The 3 facets of facilities management

Perhaps the most significant factor both underlying and driven by the fm change phenomenon has been the recognition of the need to develop the strategic side of the discipline. Back in the dark ages – say the early 1980's! – facilities managers were too pre-occupied with fire-fighting (figuratively speaking) to have the time to plan ahead so as to avoid those very same fires which stopped them planning ahead to avoid the fires which . . . and so on. In fact, the predicament was overcome by accident when a scenario arrived which threatened facilities managers' very jobs. The culprit (or the saviour as it has inadvertently turned out) was outsourcing.

Outsourcing, or the handing over of tasks and the management thereof to outside contractors, was thrown into the arena by finance directors who believed that in-house teams must be inefficient and contractors were bound to do better. In many cases they had a point. Some of the earliest fm outsourcing operations were accompanied by almost total abandonment of an in-house fm presence but it soon became apparent that organisations needed people in-house to look after their interests – not just in dealing with contractors but also in deciding what facilities were needed and what levels of performance they should aim for.

Fig. C – (from Facilities Economics) illustrates the way facilities management in London and many other UK commercial centres has polarised into three distinctive but inter-dependent facets – sponsorship, intelligence and services management.

Fig C - *Three facets of Facilities Management*

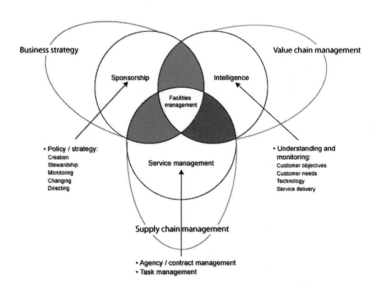

All state-of-the art facilities operations involve all three facets. Although the service management is capable of being carried out by either contractors or in-house staff – often a mixture of both – the sponsorship and intelligence must always, by definition, belong exclusively in-house.

Facilities **sponsorship** is the essence of the Intelligent/Informed Client Function (ICF); it emerges more clearly as a smaller – but critical – separately identifiable function as responsibility for facilities service management is devolved from in-house to external resources. In the less devolved, hybrid models the sponsorship role is not usually a separate function other than for capital projects where it is well established.

The term sponsorship in respect of facilities implies the ownership of responsibility for the facilities provision, the stewardship of the organisation's policy for the provision, maintenance and allocation of resources for the accommodation and services required to facilitate corporate objectives.

The 'intelligence' facet is actually both introspective and outward looking: introspective as the eyes and ears of the facilities management function with regard to core business needs and outward-looking in respect of the effectiveness of service delivery (see below) and new techniques and technology available in its support.

The sponsorship and intelligence functions of facilities management together constitute the Intelligent Client Function (ICF) which is the key to successful facilities management. Sponsorship and intelligence are unquestionably 'core' activities (ie: they directly contribute to the productive output) even though some facilities service management firms offering 'partnering' arrangements will suggest they can cope with these aspects as well. In best practice regimes the 'intelligent client' facets need to be identified and separately established in-house regardless of the location of **services management**.

It is most important to understand clearly the distinction between the line management of a particular service or task (such as 'cleaning' or 'distribution' and the overall direction and co-ordination of all the services which is defined here as 'facilities services management'. Both the individual service tasks and the facilities services management contribute to facilities services delivery but the relationships via which this is effected are many and various, as are their economic implications.

The responsibility for making the three facets gel together is with the ICF. A critical point of contact is the liaison between the facilities sponsor and the facilities services manager ie: the managing agent or contractor responsible for co-ordinating the work of the task contractors or in-house providers.

As Fig. C shows the value is generated by the intelligence and sponsorship roles with the supply chain adding to this value through the cost-efficiency of the operation.

The value chain runs via the 'intelligence' facet spanning the knowledge bases of both the user and the service provider. The supply chain is the implementation of the requirements of the facilities policy and value is added here by a cost-efficient method of services delivery which is, of course, highly dependent upon good communications right along the chain.

The recognition of this distinction between **cost-efficiency**, ie: paying the **right price**, and **cost-effectiveness** which means buying the **right thing** for the right price is critical to the success of the modern facilities management operation.

Value management

Neither the supply chain nor the value chain can operate satisfactorily unless the Intelligent Client Function is given a formal identity, totally separated from hands-on service delivery, and is staffed at a meaningful level of experience, ability and numerical strength.

Although normally a by-product of the outsourcing process the creation of the ICF in the form described here is just as applicable – indeed essential – to facilities operated fully or partially in-house.

It is the ICF which draws up the 'balanced scorecard' relating facilities performance to core business requirements although not always within the classic framework laid down by Kaplan and Norton*.

The 'Balanced Scorecard' is a general management concept, again emanating from the USA, which begs application to facilities management. In its simplest context it is concerned with creating a series of inter-relating performance management systems which seamlessly link strategy with action. These are applied throughout every facet of an organisation's activities to produce a transparent, *holistic action plan for delivering the business strategy. It addresses issues of:

- financial success
- customer satisfaction
- internal procedures
- learning and growth

The 'Balanced Scorecard' approach to these issues is to develop a management scenario in which each activity in the business addresses these four issues in the context of their contribution to the overall business strategy – which in turn is focussed at the highest level on the same four components. 'Transparency' is a key word and is used in the sense that every employee and every department has a scorecard that can be seen clearly to address the needs of the corporate plan.

The good thing, from this author's point of view, about the 'Balanced Scorecard' is that it supports the principles of relating facilities policy to the corporate plan first put down on paper in 1984 in 'Premises Audits' and expanded on in 'Facilities Economics' – first in 1994 and now, again in 2001.

Taking the four generic issues in turn we can see that:

Financial success as a corporate goal must be reflected in the cost-efficiency of the services provided and their cost-effectiveness in their contribution to corporate efficiency.

Customer satisfaction is a critical part of the facilities management role: identifying user needs and applying the services to match is one aspect of that role and another is helping to provide a good image to the external customers in respect of the buildings and services; the latter is a business marketing contribution the importance of which is frequently overlooked by facilities and general management alike. The direct effectiveness of the strategy can be measured by user satisfaction surveys and other key output performance indicators (KOPI's) but the indirect effectiveness is a 'soft' component of the profit centre.

Internal procedures in facilities terms are represented by specifications and service levels the efficiency of which, in turn, is measured using key input performance indicators (KIPI's). Such procedures have to be relevant to the output sought in support of user efficiency, **which is why the creation of specification in isolation from a business case evaluation offends fundamentally against the transparency and holisticity of the Balanced Scorecard approach.** The application of this principle in a value management context is further considered below.

And finally there is **learning and growth** which is very much the province of the Intelligent Customer whose job its to find out what facilities and service levels the business needs (intelligence = learning) and to generate, sponsor and monitor the procedures and resources needed to deliver them

It is suggested that this particular process is a function of value management as illustrated in Fig D.

Fig D – *The value management process*

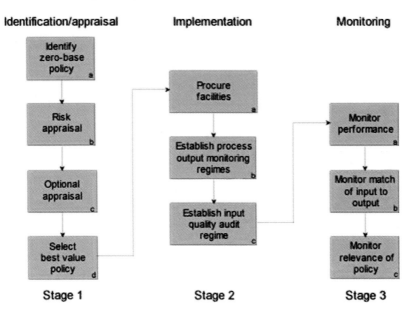

Identification/appraisal   Implementation   Monitoring

Identify zero-base policy ₐ

Risk appraisal ᵇ

Optional appraisal ᶜ

Select best value policy ᵈ

Procure facilities ₐ

Establish process output monitoring regimes ᵇ

Establish input quality audit regime ᶜ

Monitor performance ₐ

Monitor match of input to output ᵇ

Monitor relevance of policy ᶜ

Stage 1   Stage 2   Stage 3

Whether we are considering buildings or facilities services the process of value management is in principle the same. Fig. D illustrates the consecutive and cyclical order of the three facets of value management and the activities within each one.

Stage 1 represents the process of identifying a facilities requirement and the optimum level of quality and cost to be adopted in the facilities policy.

The policy having been settled Stage 2 begins with the procurement of the facility which must be accompanied by strategies for measuring input and output performance.

Stage 3 is the measurement process which includes the ongoing requirement to make sure that changed circumstances are always detected and reflected in changed strategies where necessary – thereby completing the cyclical nature of the whole process.

If the latter procedures are followed in regard to all key facilities then the principles of the 'Balanced Scorecard' will have been fully met including the all-important requirement for strategy and action to be seamless.

The business case for investment in facilities discussed above has to come from the Intelligent Customer by default – few financial directors understand the 'Balanced Scorecard' in a facilities management context. It is unfortunate that financial management is pre-occupied with 'hard' returns which are often produced on paper (artificially but not genuinely) by cutting down on the costs of so-called 'non-core' activities.

In times of recession, such as we are currently facing, pressures to reduce the fm budget can be inexorable. The term 'affordability' is frequently bandied about as if quality of support were something to switch on and off according to funds yet with no appreciable impact on the core business. If this were so then the identification/ appraisal process at Fig D above obviously could not have been implemented.

Valid savings may be sought (and sometimes made) by outsourcing although if this results in the loss of an effective Intelligent Customer Function then the learning and growth facet of the 'Balanced Scorecard' approach will be missing from the facilities operation.

Setting up the Balanced Scorecard

Wherever possible the performance criteria for the individual scorecards should be created by the individual departments and their individual employees. People must identify the critical processes at which they must excel if they are to meet the onus upon them to support the business strategy. They must then set their own targets and means of measurement – ie: key performance indicators – and even measure their own results, although inherent human frailties may require some external monitoring of achievements!

The Intelligent Client Function (ICF)

The origins of the ICF syndrome in outsourcing were discussed earlier. Today, in London, there are few organisations of any size or stature which do not have this function properly established and staffed with high-grade, well qualified, facilities management professionals.

Fig. E is the residual in-house structure where management of a public sector organisation's facilities comprising some 50,000 sq m in ten buildings was outsourced to a managing agent. Although a little top-heavy (the diagram shows the original set-up immediately post-outsourcing) the structure has proved highly cost-effective with sustained levels of improvement in performance and value for money over a five-year period.

Fig E – ICF structure – large headquarters estate

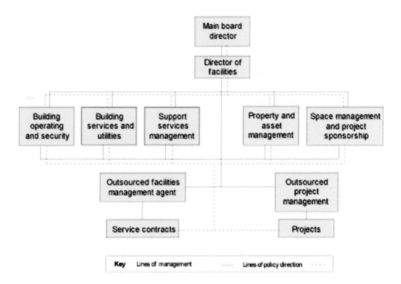

Regardless of the shape of the network it is imperative that strategic responsibility for the overall function lies within the organisation, that the personnel entrusted with sponsoring that responsibility have the appropriate levels of skill and motivation and that they have control over, and have unrestricted access to, all essential information and data (including costs) and systems.

It is extremely important to recognise that, as well as careful management of resources, the strategic role of internal facilities managers equally involves intelligence gathering; they must constantly be aware of the way the business is developing and the consequential effects on the facilities policy and the strategies in place for its delivery.

In a fully outsourced regime the residual 'intelligent client' remains the creator and guardian of the facilities policy, constantly looking inwards to the core activity, picking up signs of change to be accommodated, prompting alternative but efficient changes in procedure which will reduce and/or add value to the facilities overhead.

In a less clearly defined structure, where the internal facilities manager has some 'hands-on' services management activity, this strategic function must be recognised and given its reign (preferably independence) even amidst the hustle and bustle of day-to-day contract administration and man-management. Ideally, in the larger organisation, the facilities manager should be a Board appointment.

Managing Service Delivery

The interdependent facets of facilities management described above will these days, in London, presume some kind of outsourced solution to the problems of day-to-day service delivery.

In the early days there were many organisations who directly employed all the staff needed to run and maintain premises and business support services. It is possible that one or two examples of 100% in-house operation still exist, but probably not on a large scale. This traditional premises management function comprised engineer/technology-trained personnel in charge of a direct labour force which carried out nearly all the work except really specialist tasks such as lift maintenance.

Over the past two decades there has been a relentless move to outsourcing of one shape or another. There are two generic versions of the outsourcig approach:

- outsourcing the facilities services management ie: the direction and co-ordination of task contractors/operators

- 'out-tasking' which means contracting-out individual facilities service tasks such as cleaning and security.

The term 'out-tasking' applies whether the facilities services management is in-house or outsourced.

In the premises management arrangements of the 1980's certain of the non-engineering operations such as cleaning and security were out-tasked with tasks such as the maintenance of heating, air-conditioning and electrical services and the repair and maintenance of the 'fabric' being retained as an in-house operation.

Some organisations outsource the facilities services management and some of the tasks while holding the rest of the tasks back in-house. In these circumstances the facilities sponsor has to decide whether to transfer the direction of the in-house task teams to the facilities services manager or to retain that function in-house. The problem with the latter is that it can draw the Intelligent Customer Function into 'hands-on' management which is likely to mean that the strategic issues fail to get the individual attention they need.

On the other hand the alternative arrangement whereby in-house teams look to an external directive manager can also raise delicate issues. For instance, who assesses the employees' annual performance ratings and what redress does the external manager have for poor performance? Setting up the service-level agreement as a quasi-contract to mirror, as closely as possible, the conditions of the outsourced tasks will go a long way to reducing the extent of the problem, but in either case this uneasy split of procurement cultures is best avoided wherever possible.

The modern-day process for managing and procuring facilities services is depicted at Fig. F.

Fig. F – *Total facilities outsourcing – management contract*

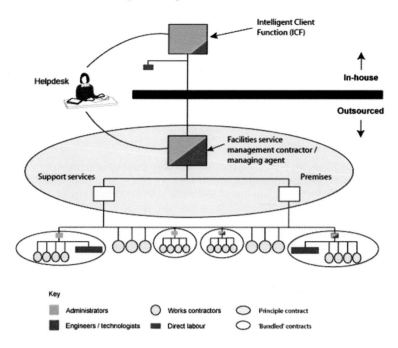

Basically it involves payment of a lump sum or percentage or sliding scale fee to a contractor or management company to organise and manage the tasks to an agreed specification and budget; the employer will sometimes enter into direct contract with the works contractors using a managing agent to co-ordinate the service provision, or the principal management contractor may interpose contractually and as the paying agent. However, in both cases the employer is committed to pay the price charged by the works contractors and is at direct risk to their default, albeit that the managing agent or management contractor will work to mitigate problems. Effectively this is the structure of so-called 'partnering' arrangements, the main difference in the latter being that the intention of the parties to work together to mutual benefit is normally expressed in a mission statement, signed by both sides but with little or no contractual significance.

One recent innovation is known as 'bundle-management' in which there is no single external facilities services manager. Instead there are groups of task contractors 'bundled' together under the overall contractual umbrella of one of their number who takes contractual responsibility for their individual and collective performance. Note that the liaison function between the facilities sponsor and each of the bundle managers becomes partly of a directive nature compared with the single point responsibility of an external facilities services management regime. Getting the balance right in the ICF to ensure that its strategic role is not compromised by too much 'hands-on' activity is make-or-break for such an arrangement.

All of these regimes require in-house management teams of varying sizes. However, the 'total management' packages need only a small kernel of core staff to liaise with the outsource partner – and some organisations believe that a simple Board Director/contractor relationship is appropriate, thereby eliminating all non-core facilities personnel. Although this may be appropriate for smaller firms, in general any failure to institute a robust 'Intelligent Client Function' is a recipe for total disaster.

Benchmarking – a key tool of value management

The ICF must establish what is best practice in terms of cost, quality and risk; benchmarking – done properly by people who know what it's about – can be a vital part of this process.

'Facilities Economics' describes benchmarking as "the process of comparing a product, service, process – indeed any activity or object – with other samples from a peer group, with a view to identifying 'best-buy' or 'best-practice' and targeting oneself to emulate it".

Benchmarking can be carried out in groups (or 'clubs') or by consultants using their own databases. In London benchmarking is a widely-used tool which is one of the main reasons why overall facilities performance is so high.

Output quality is usually benchmarked using 'customer satisfaction surveys' of the staff and also by reference to service level records from the computerised 'help-desk' functions which are now commonplace.

Before any outsourcing takes place most organisations will benchmark their facilities services to make sure they know where they stand before asking a contractor to offer any services. The same principle of using benchmark results as a springboard for developing facilities policy is usually applied to organisations setting up a new facility.

Conclusions

This has been a resume of some of the key issues influencing state-of-the-art facilities management. All of these features are available to organisations operating in the London area and it is critical to their success that they seek out facilities management personnel of the right calibre from the outset of setting up their operations.

Facilities management was once the Cinderella of business management; however Cinderella has now been to the ball and is infinitely better equipped for the next one.

Bernard Williams
September 2001

Bernard Williams Associates
Tel: 020 8460 1111
Fax: 020 8464 1167
e-mail: bernard.williams@bwassoc.co.uk
web-site: www.bwassoc.co.uk

*'The Balanced Scorecard' (Harvard Business Press)

Part 4

People, Skills and Experience

Brook Street, a National Company with a Local Market

With over 50,000 companies on our books and over half a century's experience we know that employers want the right person for the job first time and improving candidates skills to help them realise their potential is important to us.

Speak to Brook Street for all your recruitment needs.

- Temporary/Permanent Assignments
- Accounting
- Secretarial
- Contracts
- Office
- Light Industrial

Baker Street
136 Baker Street
London W1V 6FL
Tel: 020 7486 6144 Fax: 020 7935 7600
london_bakerstreet@brookstreet.co.uk

Cannon Street
131/133 Cannon Street
London EC4N 5AX
Tel: 020 7623 3966 Fax:020 7623 1401
london_cannonstreet@brookstreet.co.uk

Fenchurch Street
108 Fenchurch Street
London EC3M 5JR
Tel: 020 7481 8441 Fax: 020 7702 3069
london_fenchurchstreet@brookstreet.co.uk

Docklands
6 South Quay Plaza, 185 Marsh Wall
Isle of Dogs E14 9SH
Tel: 020 7515 8118 Fax: 020 7515 8315
docklands@brookstreet.co.uk

Holborn
230 High Holborn
Holborn, London WC1V 7DA
Tel: 020 7242 6991 Fax: 020 7405 3889
london_holborn@brookstreet.co.uk

Oxford Street
353 Oxford Street
London W1R 1FA
Tel: 020 7493 8531 Fax: 020 7493 4632
london_oxfordstreet@brookstreet.co.uk

Victoria
139 Victoria Street
London SW1E 6RD
Tel: 020 7630 6112 Fax:020 7834 2316
london_victoriastreet@brookstreet.co.uk

Strand
32 Strand
London WC2N 5HY
Tel: 020 7930 7399 Fax: 020 7839 2274
london_strand@brookstreet.co.uk

www.brookstreet.co.uk

BROOK STREET

(emp agy)

Brook Street Bureau PLC is one of the longest established recruitment agencies in Britain, founded in 1946 by Margery Hurst. From the first office situated opposite Claridge's Hotel in London, Brook Street handled seven assignments a week during its first year with 36 temporaries on its books. Today the industry as a whole has an annual turnover of more than 10 billion and is Britain's second largest employer – second only to the Government – managing employment of nearly one million people each day.

Brook Street have constantly maintained their position at the forefront of the competitive recruitment industry, whilst expanding to become a national provider of multi-disciplined employment services. If you are seeking advice on recruitment methods or staffing issues, Brook Street can help.

With over half a century's experience in recruitment we undertake to demonstrate an understanding of a client's business to ensure we deliver a tailor-made service. Our research tells us that your expectations of a recruitment agency are to spend time with an experienced professional, friendly consultant who will offer an honest assessment and evaluation of opportunities that are open to your company.

At Brook Street we have dedicated consultants whose focus is in the recruitment of permanent and temporary applicants. We understand employers want the right person for the job first time. We are an equal opportunities employer and thoroughly interview and reference all applicants before they are made available to work and we continuously assess the abilities of both our candidates and consultants. We acknowledge the importance of improving our candidates' skills to help them realise their potential. As part of our commitment to further help applicants' skills we provide free software training, using the latest computer based technology, to retain and enhance their skill levels.

Our relationship with our clients and applicants alike is of paramount importance, therefore we always make contact at the start, during and end of each assignment to discuss the experience and quality of our service. Client feedback on our applicants is essential in developing our service and customer relationship.

Our specialist knowledge of certain market sectors enables Brook Street to deliver an efficient and expert service to our clients. Our core business is the supply of temporary, permanent and contract staff with all skill types for commercial and industrial placements, including everything from secretarial and administration, to technical and production line work.

Very few agencies can boast at having a branch in every major city in the UK. We provide a 24 hour service – 365 days a year and completely free of charge, computerised training and assessment for all clients and applicants. At Brook Street UK Ltd., it's all part of the service.

4.1

An Employment Law Guide for Overseas Investors

Jonathan Exten-Wright,
DLA

Introduction

This chapter briefly outlines the basic employment law rights which any potential overseas investor should consider when deciding to do business in the UK. It will primarily deal with employees unless it is stated that separate provisions also apply to workers. European Union legislation has increasingly broadened protection beyond the narrow category of employees to the wider sense of workers, ie to all except those who are self-employed and in business on their own account.

Employees in the UK derive rights from their contracts of employment, statute and European Union law. Employees who believe their statutory employment rights have been infringed can bring a case before an employment tribunal and usually receive compensation.

The principal features of a contract of employment

Who is an employee?

It is important to make a distinction between an employee and a self-employed person as the legal rights enjoyed by each differ. An employee is an individual who has entered into, or works under, a contract of employment with an employer. A contract of employment means a contract of service or of apprenticeship. If the individual is not an employee, the work will be performed under a contract for services.

An employer cannot, however, circumvent his statutory duties merely by labelling the relationship as something else: the courts will investigate the facts to make their own finding.

Contract of employment

Most employers usually give their employees a written contract of employment when employment commences. Statute requires that as a minimum, written particulars of key terms of employment are given to an employee, often for convenience incorporated into the contract, within 13 weeks of the start date of employment.

Restrictive covenants

A restrictive covenant is a contractual agreement between an employer and an employee which protects business interests and confidential information by placing restrictions on an employee's activities both during and/or after employment. Restrictive covenants can be justified only if they go no further than is necessary to protect an employer's legitimate business interests and if they are reasonable.

Continuous employment

It should be noted that many of the individual employment rights set out in this chapter depend on an employee having worked a qualifying period of continuous employment with his or her present employer.

Unlawful deductions from wages

Employees are protected against having unauthorised deductions made from their wages. For a deduction to be lawful it must be required by legislation, or authorised by the worker's contract or consented to by the worker in writing.

The National Minimum Wage (NMW)

There is a general minimum level of £3.70 an hour for all workers subject to the following exceptions:

- £3.20 an hour for 18–21 year olds;
- £3.20 an hour for workers of 22 years and over for six months after starting a new job if they are receiving accredited training.

There are detailed rules on time for which the NMW is payable and strict limits on including the value of benefits.

Notice of termination

Both the employer and the employee are entitled to a statutory minimum period of notice of termination of employment. After one month's employment, an employee must give at least one week's notice. An employer must give an employee at least one week's notice after one month's employment, two weeks after two years, three weeks after three years and so on up to a maximum of twelve weeks, after twelve years or more. The contract of employment may always provide for a longer period of notice than the statutory minimum.

Wrongful dismissal

Where an employee is wrongfully dismissed ie without notice or with insufficient notice, the employee can bring a claim for wrongful dismissal, for the whole notice period or the remainder of the period which is unpaid. Such claims can be brought in the employment tribunal where the value of the claim does not exceed £25,000. Where the value exceeds £25,000 either all or the balance of the claim must be made in the civil courts.

International considerations

Employment of foreign nationals

The Asylum and Immigration Act 1996 makes it a criminal offence to employ a person aged 16 or over who does not have permission to live or work in the UK. The maximum penalty for this offence is £5000. Accordingly, if it is proposed that an overseas executive supervises the establishment of UK-based business, their right to enter and remain should be checked.

Employment outside the UK

Employees who ordinarily work outside Great Britain may still qualify for protection under UK employment legislation. There are detailed rules and the Courts decide which national law should apply and which national court should hear any dispute.

Posted Workers Directive

This Directive ensures that workers posted from one member state of the European Economic Area (EEA) to work in another member state are given the same employment rights as workers in the member state to which they have been posted. Employers in one member state will not be able to employ workers from another member state on terms and conditions inferior to those guaranteed by the law in the host state.

Key statutory employment rights

Unfair dismissal

An employee with at least one year's continuous service can claim unfair dismissal.

Once a dismissal is established, the employer must show the dismissal was for one of five specified reasons, namely: conduct, capability, redundancy, a legal reason which prevents the employment being continued, or 'some other substantial reason' which could justify the dismissal. The employer must then show that the reason was sufficient for dismissal, and that the process was fair.

If the dismissal was unfair, the tribunal can order one of three possible remedies:

- reinstatement to the old job;
- re-engagement to another job but on the same terms and conditions as the former job;
- compensation which is capped at a maximum of £58,900.

An order for reinstatement/re-engagement can lift the latter cap. Where an employer refuses to comply with an order for reinstatement or re-engagement, a further additional award can be made of up to 26 to 52 weeks' pay.

Redundancy

Redundancy situations arise where there is (a) closure of the business (b) a closure of the employee's workplace or (c) a diminishing need for employees to do work of a particular kind. Where redundancies of twenty or more employees are proposed, employers are required to conduct collective consultation with appropriate employee representatives.

Employers are required to make lump sum compensation payments called redundancy payments to employees dismissed through redundancy. The amount is related to the employee's age, length of continuous service with the employer, and weekly pay, up to a maximum weekly pay currently capped at £240.

Transfer of a business or undertaking

The Transfer of Undertakings (Protection of Employment) Regulations 1981 (as amended) apply to the transfer of an undertaking or part of an undertaking to a new employer (for example to the sale of an undertaking or a part of that undertaking) apart from share sales. Employees employed by the old employer at the time of the transfer automatically become the employees of the new employer as if their contracts of employment were originally made with the new employer. The new employer takes over all the employment liabilities of the old employer with the exception of criminal liabilities and, currently, occupational pension rights.

Employees must consult collectively with appropriate employee representatives about the transfer. A transfer-connected dismissal would be considered automatically unfair for those with one year's service, except in limited circumstances. Transfer-connected variations to employment terms will generally be void.

Working Time regulations

These regulations provide workers with the following minimum rights:

- A maximum working week of an average of 48 hours over a 17-week referenced period, although the worker may opt out of these arrangements.
- A right to at least four weeks' paid leave per year.
- A right to eleven consecutive hours' rest in any 24 hour period.
- A right to a rest break after six hours.
- A right to one day off each week.
- A limit on the normal working hours of night workers to an average of eight hours in any 24-hour period and an entitlement for night workers to receive regular health assessments.

These Regulations apply both to employees and workers.

Equal pay

Employers must afford equal pay to men and women who are employed on like work, work rated as equivalent under a job evaluation study, or work found to be of equal value.

Fixed term contracts

A fixed term contract is a contract for a specific stated term fixed in advance which can be ascertained in advance by reference to some relevant circumstances ie the end is identified by a precise date in the future. Regulation is anticipated shortly. The Fixed Term Workers Directive must be implemented in the UK by 10 July 2001 to protect fixed term workers against discrimination. It also regulates the circumstances in which fixed term contracts can be used, their duration, their frequency and prevents abuse arising from the use of successive fixed term contracts.

Part-time workers

The Part-Time Workers (Prevention of Less Favourable Treatment) Regulations 2000

These regulations give part-time workers the right not to be treated less favourably in their terms and conditions than comparable full-time workers unless the treatment can be justified. The regulations cover part-time employees, working under a contract of employment and workers who are not genuinely self-employed working part-time for a business. This could include agency workers or workers on a fixed term contract.

Non-discrimination

Sex and race discrimination

Under the Sex Discrimination Act 1975 (SDA), it is unlawful for employers to discriminate on grounds of sex, marital status or against anyone intending to undergo, undergoing or who has undergone gender reassignment.

The Race Relations Act 1976 (RRA) makes discrimination by employers on racial grounds unlawful, ie discrimination on grounds of race, colour, nationality (including citizenship) or ethnic or national origins.

These Acts prohibit discrimination by employers against job applicants, existing employees, contract agency workers and the self-employed.

Disability discrimination

The Disability Discrimination Act 1995 (DDA)

It is unlawful for employers with fifteen or more employees to discriminate against current or prospective employees with disabilities and people who have had a disability. A disability is defined as a physical or mental impairment which has a substantial and long-term adverse affect on the ability to carry out normal day to day activities. The impairment is long-term if it lasts, or is likely to last, for at least twelve months. Discrimination occurs when for reasons related to the present disability, an employer treats a disabled person less favourably than he treats or would treat other people and cannot justify this treatment. It also occurs where an employer fails to comply with the duty to make reasonable adjustments in relation to the disabled person and that failure cannot be justified.

Family friendly rights

Maternity

Time off for ante-natal Care
At present, employees are entitled to time off with pay to keep appointments for ante-natal care made on the advice of a registered medical practitioner, midwife or health visitor.

Ordinary maternity Leave
At present an employee is entitled to 18 weeks ordinary maternity leave regardless of the length of service. The woman can choose to start maternity leave at any time from 11th week before the expected week of childbirth. During the 18 weeks' leave, a woman is entitled to benefit from all of her normal terms and conditions of employment except for remuneration. Women who wish to return to work before the end of their ordinary maternity leave must give 21 days' notice.

Additional maternity Leave
Employees who have completed one year's continuous service with their employer by the 11th week before the expected week of confinement are entitled to an additional period of leave. This is up to 29 weeks beginning with the week in which the childbirth occurred.

Statutory maternity pay (SMP)
A woman is entitled to SMP if she has worked for her employer for a continuous period of at least 26 weeks ending with the 15th week before the expected week of childbirth, and has average weekly earnings of at least equal to the lower earnings limit for National Insurance contributions. SMP can be paid for up to 18 weeks and it is payable by the employer but partly reimbursed by the state.

Parental leave

Employees who have completed one year's service with their employer are entitled to 13 weeks' unpaid parental leave for each child born or adopted on or after 15 December 1999. The right applies to parents and to a person who has obtained legal parental responsibility for a child.

Collective rights – trade unions

Compulsory trade union recognition

Unions can be recognised (or derecognised) on a compulsory basis for collective bargaining purposes where there is a sufficient majority of the workers comprising the relevant bargaining unit.

Trade union membership

An employee cannot be refused employment for being a member of a trade union or for proposing to become such a member, or for not belonging to a trade union.

Time off work for trade union duties and activities

An employee who is an official of an independent trade union which is recognised by the employer must be allowed reasonable time off with pay during working hours.

Industrial action

There is no right to strike in the United Kingdom and this has important consequences for both individuals and trade unions.

Trade unions calling for industrial action may be committing one or more various civil wrongs. A trade union, however, has statutory immunity from certain liabilities, for example, if (a) the action is official, where the majority have voted in favour of such action in a secret ballot of the workforce; and (b) that any picketing is lawful.

New Trends in Working Practices

Keith Faulkner,
Manpower

The London of the new millennium, in terms of working practices, is radically different from the London of the past. Many of what were considered to be traditional ways of working from the last fifty years have disappeared – and those that have remained have been altered beyond recognition. The trend is now towards secure flexibility – offering scope for employees and considerable benefits for business.

So what factors have created this change?

Demographics

While the 'nine-to-five, five-days-a-week' is still dominant, it is being steadily superseded by a more dynamic working environment. Changes in the demographics of the workforce have been the driving factor. The employment of older people, re-skilling of people so they can work in non-traditional industries and the provision of flexibility for women returning to work after having had children have all been necessary to address skills shortages in a tightening labour market. The result is an adaptable workforce with highly transferable skills – making London an ideal location for new businesses as well as traditional industries undergoing change.

Younger people are holding senior positions in many of London's businesses – partly the result of the dot.com boom that was centred in the City – and this is encouraging the consolidation/normalisation of new working trends. Home working, flexible hours and improved work-life balance are all recognised as necessary factors, which have improved, not harmed London's workforce. A very large proportion now work from home on at least an occasional basis.

Technology

One of the biggest changes to the way we work has been the emergence of the virtual office. The development of the Internet, laptop computers and mobile phones now mean that it is possible to be away from the office, but still be able to work as effectively. This has resulted in a huge rise in the number of home-workers, which now consists of 5.5 per cent of the British workforce.

Infrastructure

At the same time, there are infrastructural developments, with new houses and offices being built in the Docklands and a number of inner London areas being targeted for regeneration schemes. The Docklands development is encouraging greater commuting from the South East of London, effectively releasing the potential of a new workforce, while the regeneration of inner London areas ensures that London retains a base of residential workers rather than being entirely dependent on commuters.

Training & development

In addition to physical developments in London's infrastructure there are also a number of initiatives in London to target people with actual or latent skills who currently face barriers to employment, but who, with the right encouragement and support, can make a contribution to filling gaps in employer's requirements. Examples of this include older workers, lone parents, graduates uncertain of their place in the market, and people with some form of disability.

Manpower chairs the London Chamber of Commerce Skills & Employment Forum, which is helping business and government work in partnership to tackle these issues and provide training and work for all. The Forum is typical of numerous business-led initiatives in London and was launched in June 2000. It comprises fifty senior business people with a particular interest and expertise in finding practical solutions to the problem of skills shortages in the capital, building better links between business and education, and influencing politicians and decision-makers on skills and employment issues. The three main issues currently being addressed are Business-Education; Skills: Recruitment and Retention in a Tight Labour Market, and Employment Legislation.

The Forum also includes representatives from higher and further education and from key partner organisations such as the Employment Service. Effective lines of communication have been established between the Forum and the London Development Agency and links are being built with the London LSCs.

Other Government-led initiatives include the use of Individual Learning Accountants (ILAs), which help employees pay for work-related training, by providing discounts on courses and encouraging employer contributions. In 1999–2000, nearly 3000 people applied for ILAs, and this is expected to grow to over 11,000 in 2000–2001.

Trade Unions have also played a significant part in the development of workforce skills. The TUC has launched an initiative called *Bargaining for Skills*, which aims to 'put learning back on the workplace agenda'. It provides courses to assist trade union representatives in promoting the benefits of learning and in assessing the training needs of their members.

Investor in People (IIP) was launched ten years ago, and has been widely recognised as an accreditation for organisations with a genuine commitment to developing their workforce. Since then there has been a marked increase in the level of employer investment in the training and development of the workforce. Investors in People provides a framework for developing the workforce in line with business objectives, and many companies can attest to the effectiveness of this policy. To become an 'Investor In People' a company must satisfy a number of criteria, including showing the organisation is committed to supporting the development of its people, that people are encouraged to improve their own and other people's performance, and that people believe their contribution to the organisation is recognised. A large number of well-recognised companies are now involved in the scheme, including Sainsburys and TNT.

Evidence of the shift in employer behaviour comes from the CBI's Employment Trends series; employers are increasingly recognising that raising employee and management skills is the key to increasing competitiveness, with over 50 per cent of employers regarding workforce and management skills as key, both now and in five years time. The report also shows that almost 50 per cent of employees are currently training beyond the needs of their job, and a further 22 per cent are considering doing so in the future.

This has also been shown in the numbers of companies that now have policies to promote employability. Another recent survey from the CBI showed that 66 per cent of companies offered support for independent study, and 55 per cent gave time off for independent study. In addition to this, 52 per cent of companies had introduced employee development programmes, while a further 28 per cent of respondents were considering doing so.

Another feature of the London labour market is that it has high concentrations of ethnic groups in specific areas and these communities often also have under-utilised talent pools where issues of confidence or language can be an easily removed block on progress. It is hoped that closer links between employers and community-based organisations, the expansion of employee development programmes and improved job prospects will be able to overcome this by improving the skills of these under utilised workers.

In July 1999, Central London Partnership and FOCUS Central London published the first *Skills Action Plan for Central London*. This proposed a vision of Central London as a place where people and businesses treat skills as their number one priority affecting both their competitiveness and prosperity. As part of this, extensive research was carried out, and a number of forecasts made:

- the numbers employed will increase by 113,000 between 2000 and 2010;
- the level of part-time employment is expected to increase, mainly filled by women, while the level of full time male employment is expected to decrease;
- the skills of the workforce are adapting to the needs of a knowledge-based economy.

London benefits from a high concentration of resources in support of the labour market in terms of voluntary, not for profit, and private and public sector agencies providing training and support. The formation of the Learning and Skills Councils (five covering the Greater London area) will also ensure better co-ordination and direction of educational activity to underpin the continued development of the local labour market.

Another beneficial feature is that employers in London are supported by a highly developed private sector agency network and one of the most flexible legislative regimes in Europe, at the forefront of flexible working practices. Job share, teleworking, flexible working hours and a sophisticated use of temporary, contract and interim staff and managers all contribute to encouraging a highly efficient use of human resources. This is supported by a labour force who have actively embraced the freedoms and variety that more flexible approaches to work and career development can bring. Intel recently carried out a three-month pilot scheme to introduce flexible working practices. Employees were encouraged by their managers to work from home one to two days a week. Following this, questionnaires were sent out to those involved, and the verdict was that 80 per cent felt the scheme improved their work-life balance.

With the developments across London, through both the improvement of its infrastructure, and the expansion of business education, the London labour market is set to grow. And it is because of, not despite the many and varied challenges it faces, that London has emerged as one of the world's most flexible and dynamic labour markets. Despite suffering skills shortages in some sectors (31 per cent of employers reported it difficult to fill vacancies in 1999, according to the *Skills Action Plan 2000 – A Workforce Development Plan for Central London*) and facing continuing infrastructure difficulties, the market remains buoyant. Manpower's Quarterly Survey of Employment Prospects showed that every business sector in London was expecting to take on more staff during the third quarter in 2001, despite talk of economic slowdown.

London is ideally placed to benefit from having a highly flexible workforce, as the UK has few restrictions on use of flexible working patterns. A quarter of the UK workforce are now employed on a part-time basis. In 1996, only 12 per cent of part-time employees worked part-time because they could not find a new job; 71 per cent preferred to work part-time. Despite this, it is still predominately women who work part-time, with nearly half doing so, compared with just 9 per cent of men. There are also around 8 per cent of all workers employed on a temporary basis, their numbers having increased throughout the 1990s, while the numbers of casual and seasonal staff have fallen.

Two studies throw further light on the move to greater workforce flexibility. Many employers offer flexible working time patterns, according to the 1999 CBI/Mercer Employment Trends Survey. Nearly half of all employers used shift work, with 40 per cent allowing flexible working hours, and around 10 per cent using term-time working and annualised hours arrangements.

According to the Institute for Employment Studies (IES), there are 1.5 million people working from home (5.5 per cent of the British workforce). The business and financial services industries in particular have seen a remarkable growth, with over a quarter of all teleworkers coming from this sector.

The IES also discovered that there is a social factor to consider with teleworking. It showed that, compared with the rest of the working population, flexible workers are more likely to be of graduate calibre, to be married and to be in mid-career. Younger employees enjoy working and interacting with colleagues. The isolation and loneliness which can occur by working from home can act as a deterrent to younger lower-level workers, while for the same reasons invites older, senior employees to adopt such practices because of their settled social and family life.

The experience of teleworkers can vary enormously with age and experience. There is the issue of senior managers being very good at working flexibly as their experience has equipped them with better time management and organisational skills, skills which younger employees have not had time to develop fully.

Ursula Huwes, Associate Fellow of the IES, commented: 'With one British worker in seventeen now using the new technology to work from home, teleworking is reaching critical mass. The time has come for some joined-up thinking about the implications of this development for housing policy, transport policy, employment policy and the quality of individual working experience and family life. If it continues to expand in a piecemeal fashion there is a real danger of some sections of society being left out.'

Recruitment agencies also have an important role to play in the further development of London as an international business centre. The use of flexible staffing will continue to develop with a growing use of 'staffing solutions' whereby specialist agencies provide cost-effective, output-priced service, integrated into the user's own business structure – a form of virtual company where a collaboration between a variety of individuals and suppliers ensures business results finely tuned to the changing demands of the market.

London now has the resources, the mechanisms to deliver improving skills and benefits from a vibrancy that continues to attract talented people to the capital from across Europe and the world. With its continuing development and regeneration of areas such as the Docklands and East London, there will be a pool of talent from which new workers can be drawn to further economic expansion. The continued development should also provide housing suitable for young professional or middle management staff working in London.

The gradual improvement in the transport infrastructure should also allow for easier commuting both to and across London, further boosting the labour market. These developments, coupled with government initiatives such as IIP, the creation of Individual Learning Accounts, and the development of flexible working practices means there will be a skilled pool of talent from which international companies based in and around London will be able to draw to ensure they get the right staff. In addition, the wealth of experience possessed by recruitment agencies such as Manpower will further ensure companies are able to meet their recruitment targets, and match staffing levels closely to output requirements.

Sources
Labour Market – Quarterly Report November 2000
CBI – Employment Trends Survey 2000
CBI – Creating a Europe that works
Employment Policy Foundation – Workplace Policy for the New Economy
Employment Policy Foundation – Sound Employment Policy for the Twenty First Century
Focus Central London – Annual Report April 1999 – March 2000
Focus Central London – Skills Action Plan 2000
Manpower – Quarterly Survey of Employment Prospects
Economic and Social Research Council – Agenda
Getting London working – Single Regeneration Budget Bid Round 5

4.3

London's Workforce and its Skills

Keith Faulkner,
Manpower

Labour and skills shortages have been two of the toughest issues facing London businesses over the last few years. A strong economy, increasingly focusing on the capital, has often meant that servicing – rather than winning – business has been the challenge for London-based firms.

In some areas, such as IT, skills shortage has restricted the growth of some businesses. However, because recruitment experts, including employers, agencies and government, have anticipated the issue for a while, plans are in place to manage this – and the benefits of these are already being seen.

The London Development Agency (LDA) is central to this work. The LDA has identified nine priorities for ensuring London's economy continues to grow and the workforce has the skills necessary to help fuel this expansion. This draft economic strategy includes:

- promoting London as a place for people and business;
- sustaining the London city region;
- meeting London's key challenges;
- improving business competitiveness;
- encouraging economic diversity;
- **prioritising knowledge and learning;**
- empowering London's communities, and helping disadvantaged people into work;
- developing the sustainable world city;
- strengthening London's capacity to deliver at the economic development arm of the new London institutions.

Although London has the most highly skilled workforce in the country, both the public and private sectors are taking steps to further develop the already wide range of skills possessed by London's workforce. Both sectors have acknowledged that the continued development of the workforce's skills is paramount, with the LDA rating it as one of the top priorities for London. With the highest concentrations of Higher Education Centres in the UK, including 28 universities, 12 higher education colleges and 56 further education colleges, offering over 25,000 courses available to study, London is already well-placed to develop the skills of its workforce.

London has developed as a major international centre, particularly with regards to the City of London, which by March 2001 had attracted 481 foreign banks, totalling more than any other centre world-wide. London also has the one of the world's largest fund management centres, international insurance, derivatives trading, security dealing, legal services, accountancy, management consulting, and the largest foreign exchange market in the world, accounting for 32 per cent of global turnover in 1998, showing the level of international experience which exists in a key sector such as financial services. This sector now accounts for 43 per cent of London's GDP, and employs approximately 900,000 people.

With regards to the language skills available, London is ideally placed to support any pan-European business. London has a huge number of people with one or more additional languages, so companies that regularly deal with customers and businesses across Europe would find it considerably easier to recruit staff, than if they were established in other locations around the country. Typical of the international businesses doing this is Delta Airlines, which decided to consolidate its 14 European-wide contact centres into one in West London. Mike Boynton, Regional Director for Reservations Sales Europe, commented: 'We had no difficulties in recruiting staff equipped with language skills of mother-tongue standard for each of the 14 countries that Delta's London contact centre now represent.'

According to figures from London's Local Education Authorities, there are now 300 different languages spoken in the homes of London's schoolchildren. Almost one-third of all London schoolchildren have a language other than English as their first. This variety of languages, spoken by so many children, provides a huge number of additional languages for employers to draw from. In addition, the multilingual and multicultural population in London gives international firms an insight into the society behind virtually any world market, and the prospect of using staff who can not only communicate with any of those markets, but also have some understanding as to how and why they function. Research has shown that London is unique in Europe in being able to provide such a large, skilled, multi-lingual labour force.

In addition to the extensive language skills available in London, there are also high levels of education compared with the rest of the UK, with almost 30 per cent of people in Inner London possessing a degree. The table below shows the percentages of economically active people of working age[1] by highest qualification achieved.

	Inner London	Outer London	UK
Degree or equivalent	29.9	17.3	13.2
Higher education below degree	7.0	8.4	9.0
GCE A Level or equivalent	18.1	23.5	26.3
GCSE or equivalent	11.8	18.4	18.7
Other qualifications	17.8	17.6	15.6
No qualifications	15.0	14.5	16.9
Not known	0.4	0.3	0.3
Total economically active (000s)	1267	2106	27,614

Source: *Labour Force Survey, Office for National Statistics*

London's workforce also has a wide range of specialisations. As previously mentioned, the financial services sector is now one of the largest in the world, but London is also benefiting from growth in new sectors. Due to its close proximity to mainland Europe, and the excellent transport links to destination across the world, served by a number of international airports, plus the international rail terminal at Waterloo, London is ideally placed to allow other new sectors to expand. Many newer industries have set up, not just within London, but also within the adjacent M25 area, including global companies such as Microsoft. Many of the dot.com companies also set up in or around London, due to the particular technical skills required for creating, running and promoting a website.

Compared with the rest of the UK, London has a far higher proportion of managers and professional people than the rest of the UK. In 1995, 44.2 per cent of London's top jobs were in the top two occupational categories, compared with 34.9 per cent of the UK as a whole.

	London[2] (%)	UK (%)
Managerial and administrators	18.7	14.9
Professional, associate professional	25.5	20.0
Clerical and secretarial	19.4	16.4
Craft and related	5.9	10.1
Personal and protective services	10.8	11.6
Sales	7.8	8.6
Plant and machine operatives	5.3	10.0
Other	6.7	8.5
Total employees (000's)[3]	2633	22,553

Source: *Labour Force Survey*

Many companies newly locating in London may have difficulties in finding the right staff to recruit due to the diversity of skills, languages and a multitude of specialisations. This is where recruitment agencies such as Manpower, government bodies or the Internet have a role to play. It is now possible for a newly locating company to have all the groundwork carried out before a management presence is even established. There are three main options that exist for recruitment; the public Employment Service, private recruitment agencies and pure e-recruiters.

The public Employment Service is increasingly well-placed for major recruitment campaigns associated with large recruitment drives, such as a retail site, a substantial back office function or a manufacturing base. Unlike the services offered by the private sector recruitment agencies, the Employment Service is focused on front end recruitment, requiring a higher level of engagement from the employer and will normally only provide front end recruitment. On the positive side, they are free to use, and for this reason, many companies use the Employment Service to help them fill front-end roles.

Private sector agencies are able to provide a much wider variety of services, ranging from 'topping up' any harder to fill vacancies, such as ones that require particular skills to providing additional staff during the set up. They are also capable of supplying a fully outsourced HR function that can take over the whole challenge of getting the workforce together and managing the transition and changing skill set requirements of a business start-up.

Another option for a newly locating company would be through web-based recruitment. Web-based recruitment can prove to be an economical way of researching the market to test availability and pay rates for particular skills. Pure e-recruiters generally leave the burden of assessment, referencing and selection to their client, which can prove to be a problem if the client has limited resources to deal with this. Fortunately, most of the more established 'bricks and mortar' agencies are increasingly coupled with or include web-based recruitment facilities as part of their service.

With the recruitment and retention of staff still a business critical issue, London is ideally placed to benefit from this. With its pool of skilled, educated, multilingual and specialised workers, London is quickly becoming a prime site for foreign or pan-European business to site their offices. By locating in London, many firms are able to find all the skills they need for the modern business world. This, combined with the many advantages of living and working in London, mean the staff are easier to recruit.

Notes

[1] Working age is defined as men aged 16–64 and women aged 16—59
[2] Residents in London
[3] Includes those who did not state their occupation

4.4

Education and Training in London

For those firms wishing to locate in London standards of education are important – for employees who may be moving to London with school age children, as well as for the supply of workers. Analysis of *GCSE* results shows that they reflect spatial inequalities within the Greater London area. Boroughs showing the worst performance, in terms of the percentage of pupils gaining 5 GCSE grades between A and C, tend to have the highest levels of economic deprivation. In 1995, while 43.5 per cent of pupils in England and Wales gained 5 GCSE grades between A and C, in Islington the proportion was only 17.4 per cent – the poorest record of all 108 local education authorities in England and Wales. This poor performance reflects Islington's position as the borough with the third highest proportion of children receiving free school meals in the country.[1]

Range of attainment

This example reflects one side of London's wide range of attainment. For instance, approximately one-fifth of 15 year olds in *maintained* schools in Barking and Dagenham achieved good grades in their GCSE's, while the figure was over 50 per cent for those in Kingston-upon-Thames.[2] Thus, it is possible for employees to live in areas where maintained schools produce satisfactory results. However, the costs of locating in an area with an appropriate school are likely to be much greater than for other areas of London. For those who are willing to pay for their children's education, independent schools have pupil/teacher ratios much lower than in maintained schools and, on average, higher levels of achievement.

This picture seems unfavourable for employees and employers, even in an area that attracts a high number of well qualified individuals.

However, the disparities that exist at GCSE level tend to disappear at A level, with mean scores for London as a whole in line with those in the rest of the country. It is also the case that disparities between boroughs are greatly reduced. For instance, in 1993 Islington's below-average achievement at GCSE level was in contrast to the boroughs above-average mean score at A level.[3] Although the situation of the capital's primary and secondary education sectors is far from satisfactory, results for post-16 education are of a much higher standard. This is even more marked if we move on to one of London's most valuable assets – the higher education sector.

The higher education sector

The higher education sector in London attracts students from all over the world, as well as from the rest of the UK. The high number of foreign students who come to study in London's 13 universities and 12 colleges of higher education are part of a full-time student population of 155,000.[4] This adds to the multicultural nature of the capital's population, making London one of the few truly international cities. Workers and students from differing ethnic backgrounds may appreciate the multicultural nature of the capital's social life, while employers are able to take advantage of the 193 languages which are spoken in London.[5]

While initial qualifications are important, the concept of lifetime learning is a necessity in any major economy. It is imperative for both employers and employees to work towards a comprehensive system of skill updating through on-the-job-training. Although the UK has, in the past, faced criticism when compared to countries such as Germany, this has been reversed somewhat in recent years as the German model has come under criticism – German workers may be highly skilled but the costs of employing them seem to have become prohibitively expensive. Additionally, as the European *Labour Force Survey* shows, the UK has a better record than Germany in terms of the continuation of training throughout an individual's working life. It is encouraging to note that London's employers and employees are more willing to undertake training than their counterparts in the rest of the UK.[6] For firms wishing to recruit from the unemployed, however, a commitment to training in the initial period of employment may be a necessity.

The working age population

The relative attraction of London when compared to other global cities will depend to a large extent on the industry and stage in the production process of the firm in question. An analysis of the occupational and industrial distribution of London's working population provides an indication of the skills available to prospective firms. Furthermore, in this analysis the characteristics of the employed and unemployed are analysed separately – employers recruiting from the unemployed are likely to be paying lower wages, but higher training costs. The large number of individuals who commute from the rest of the south east (600,000 individuals living in ROSE work in Greater London – *Labour Force Survey,* 1996 Quarter 1) and the increasingly integrated nature of the whole south eastern economy necessitate the inclusion of the ROSE area in any analysis of the potential workforce.

Despite the considerable expansion of the UK's higher education sector in recent years, the proportion of 18–22 year olds in full-time education is still only half the average for the countries of the OECD.[7] However, London and the rest of the South East attract a disproportionately high percentage of these graduates – with 26 per cent of the capital's and 22 per cent of ROSE's working age population having higher education or equivalent qualifications, compared to 20 per cent for the country as a whole. If we look at only those in employment in the capital this figure rises even further to 33 per cent, while only 16 per cent of the capital's unemployed have higher education or equivalent qualifications.[8]

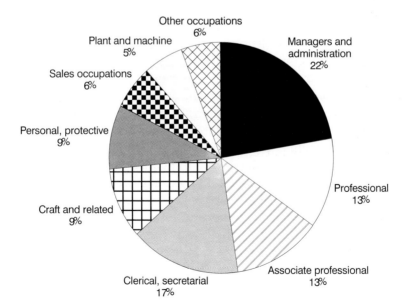

Figure 4.4.1   *Occupational distribution of employees and self-employed working in Greater London*
Source: Labour Force Survey, 1995 (first quarter)

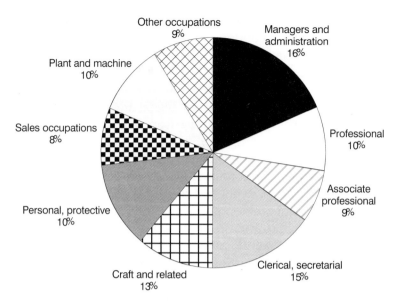

Figure 4.4.2 *Occupational distribution of employees and self-employed working in Great Britain*
Source: Labour Force Survey. 1995 (first quarter)

The local economy

As we can see from Figures 4.4.1 and 4.4.2 the local economy is strongly oriented towards higher level occupations compared to the rest of the country. Managers, administrators, professionals and associate professionals constitute 48 per cent of all those employed in Greater London. This concentration of professional services is complemented by a high proportion of clerical and secretarial workers (17 per cent of those in employment). Analysis of their previous occupations shows that 26 per cent of the capital's unemployed were in these higher occupational categories in their last job – 22 per cent for ROSE. As with those in employment a large proportion of the unemployed have clerical and secretarial skills – 15 per cent in ROSE and the capital.

Given London's role as a global financial centre, it is not surprising that over one-quarter of all the capital's employees work in the financial intermediary, real estate, renting and business services sector. The importance of information technology in such a centre of business and finance is reflected in the 48,800 individuals in 1995 employed in computer and software services.[9] However, despite 84 per cent of the workforce being in service employment, manufacturing is still an important part of the London economy. High levels of productivity in the manufacturing sector reflect a combination of high technology manufacturing, increasingly located in the rest of the South East, as well as the location of head offices in Greater London – with 16 per cent of those in employment working in manufacturing, contributing 22 per cent of London's GDP.

Job creation rates and job filling

Job creation rates have been highest for the financial intermediary, real estate, renting and business services sectors. Less than 15 per cent of the unemployed in the entire south east region are from these sectors. As one would expect the previous industry groups of the unemployed in the south east region reflect the ongoing decline of certain industries such as electrical and mechanical engineering. However, there are increasing opportunities for individuals with skills in these industries as firms involved in high technology manufacturing are attracted to the rest of the South East.

Despite there being 77,000 unemployed persons, in the Greater London area alone, who were previously employed in the professional/managerial occupations, according to an LCCI survey[10] employers are experiencing particular difficulties in filling posts in these areas. It may be that these potential employees are seen as being too old, too expensive or lacking in core abilities, such as communication skills. While this has raised the fear that skill shortages will place upward pressure on pay, the capital's economy may be in a better position to accommodate this increase in demand than many of its overseas rivals.

Conclusion

In recent years many commentators have argued that the world economy has changed to such an extent that countries can sustain consistently high rates of growth without triggering inflation – this is clearly an exaggeration.[11] However, it is likely that the labour market deregulation of the past 15 years, together with the capital's high exposure to international competition may help restrain future upward pressure on wages. Additionally, individuals who work in managerial and professional occupations have high levels of geographical mobility. It is therefore unlikely that any increase in the demand for workers, as the London economy continues to expand, will lead to a major rise in pay rates that would be detrimental to the capital's international competitiveness. The LCCI estimates that average earnings grew by 6.1 per cent in 1997 and will grow by approximately 5 per cent a year for the years 1997–2001, with productivity gains set to outstrip those in the rest of the country.[12]

Notes

[1] CENTEC/CILNTEC (now *Focus Central London*) (1996), 'Central London Economic Assessment', Research for Central London.

[2] HMSO (1995), *London Facts and Figures,* Government Office for London.

[3] ibid.

[4] Op. cit.

[5] Op. cit.

[6] *Labour Force Survey,* 1996 Quarter 1.

[7] OECD (1996), *Employment Outlook,* July, p 119.

[8] Op. cit.

[9] Central Statistical Office (now Office for National Statistics) (1995), *Annual Employment Survey.*

[10] Ibid.

[11] See *The Economist* (1997), 'Business cycles and stockmarkets', April 5–11; p 17.

[12] Op. cit.

Lifelong Learning Systems

What?

E-Learning Solutions
Over 300 online courses
E-Learning Management Systems
Learning Logs & Action Planning

Why?

To link Strategy & HRM
To work better at less cost
To develop your people
To help your business to WIN

How?

Internet access
At work, home, on the road
Designed for your needs
Secure, flexible, economical

Who?

Companies, large & small
Professional Bodies for CPD
Public sector
Education sector
Individuals

Where?

Contact LLS Ltd.
customer-service@lls.co.uk
ajones@lls.co.uk
www.lls.co.uk
www.lls.co.uk/students/

LLS, developed at Brunel University with funding from ADAPT ESFgb.

LIFELONG LEARNING SYSTEMS
e-learning solutions to suit your needs and your purse

Whatever size of your organization, you are likely to be well aware of the need to invest in your 'human capital', the talents of your people. You will also be aware that now is the time to go 'electronic' or risk economic exclusion. Lifelong Learning Systems (LLS) can help you to achieve both these goals, by linking e-learning and e-business.

To meet your needs, LLS has designed a product which is so flexible that it can cope with almost any size or type of organization, from the lone trader to the sophisticated large corporate. We provide a range of services and solutions. We are one of the few organizations nationally which sells e-learning courses to individuals and SMEs, as well as to large Corporates. It is possible to order a single LLS course online. All our courses are world–class, accredited and accessible any where in the world.

Currently we have over 300 e-courses, in IT at all levels, in Management and in Key skills. Courses can be accessed via the web and you can get into them wherever you are, at work, at home, in a training centre, on the road, at any time that suits your schedule and your lifestyle. Only e-literate companies will thrive in the e-world. And the same goes for individuals. Here's your chance to do something about it.

LLS can also offer you a way of logging and tracking all new learning and new skills and build up a record of achievement for the individual and for the organization. Our web-based System can be customized to meet your precise needs. Our 5 years experience has taught us that over-elaborate systems can be a waste of time and money. Keep it simple and able to adopt new technologies.

E-Learning is not a miracle cure. **E-Learning** is a tool, part of a blended training solution for human resource development. Companies which want to move into e-commerce cannot afford to have staff who are not confident and competent e-users. Companies go through various stages. They may start e-illiterate, become e-learners, then e-communicators, they may graduate into e-commerce, then e-business. They may develop e-HRM systems, e-CRM systems and e-Management systems. Wherever you are on this spectrum, LLS can help you to move to the next stage. You have to start somewhere so why not contact us now to find out how to take that next step?

For online courses, go to
www.lls.co.uk, contact Customer-support@lls.co.uk

For consultancy and advice, contact
Professor Anne Jones, annej@lls.co.uk

For a demo of the LLS system, contact
customer-support@lls.co.uk or 01491 57 8672

Lifelong Learning Systems
23, Queen Street, Henley-on-Thames, RG9 1AR, UK

LLS, developed at Brunel University with funding from ESFgb

4.5

R&D Facilities

For the past 20 years the UK has attracted more than 40 per cent of all inward investment into the EU. Over this period foreign firms have increasingly located not only their manufacturing but also the research, development and design of their products in the UK, making it one of Europe's prime locations for R&D operations.

When deciding on where to locate the innovator faces a set of strategic choices. A firm needs access to basic research undertaken at universities in order to investigate any commercial applicability. Although results of this are usually published in scientific journals and are therefore in the public domain, many leading university research centres enter partnerships with firms, promising either exclusive use of findings or at least a significant technological lead. Science parks bring companies and universities together and are often developed in close proximity to university sites. Firms may also try to stay ahead of competitors by employing the most distinguished experts in a particular field. Although the scientific community tends to be geographically mobile, the location of a company's R&D facilities could attract or indeed discourage potential recruits from joining the team.

A strong regional or national science base and hence the availability of young scientists is crucial for innovators, since it will assist the inflow of new ideas into the firm's existing R&D department. Additionally, firms will evaluate the investment climate which will be dependent upon the level of corporate taxation, the property market, transport facilities and the availability of investment incentives within a country or region. The following section assesses each of these factors with respect to London and the rest of the south east of England.

Basic research

Universities employ research active personnel in the hope that the papers they publish will bring distinction to their departments while attracting external funding through the government, industry or charities.

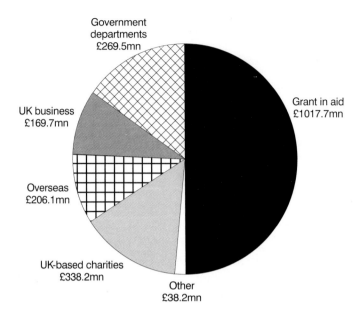

Figure 4.5.1   *R & D funding of higher education institutions, 1995–6
Source: DTI Science, Engineering and Technology Statistics, 1997*

Universities in the UK compete for government research grants, which in 1996 amounted to £1017.7 million (see Figure 4.5.1). This represents almost 50 per cent of total R&D funding for higher education. In 1996 the Higher Education Funding Councils[1] published the most recent results of the Research Assessment Exercise which is now held every 4 years. The research output of subject groups is ranked on a scale from 1 to 5+ and only universities which score 3b or higher (in 1996) receive funding through the HEFCs. Not only will money be allocated in line with achievement, the quality of research will also be made more obvious for potential partners in industry, researchers and students. These funds are not linked to specific projects, but in addition, the British government gives money to research councils, which have been set up for broad areas of research.[2] Universities (and outside research institutions) can apply for funding of particular projects through these research councils.

As we can see from Figure 4.5.1 charities account for almost 17 per cent of total R&D funding, although their contribution to medical research is far more important than in other disciplines. The third source of research funding is industry. The total industry funding of higher education institutions in the UK amounted to £169.7 million, or 8.3 per cent of the total funds available. Some institutions and faculties attract no money from private sources while others depend upon it.

In the field of science, engineering and technology research London and the rest of the South East host several institutions offering standards of international excellence. Among the most distinguished are the Imperial College of Science and Technology (London), University College London, Sussex University, Southampton University, the Cranfield Institute of Technology and Oxford University. Cambridge University, located in the neighbouring region of East Anglia, is only one hour from the centre of London.

Collaborative research

Universities seeking partnership with companies often undertake contract research or collaborative research.[3] While conducting contract research, the university neither expects to publish the results nor owns the intellectual property rights. Contract research is a service provided by the university and charged at a commercial price.

Collaborative research implies the joint definition of research goals and the undertaking of specific parts of the project by both partners. Both partners would also contribute financially to the costs of research. Ownership of intellectual property rights, publishing of results and user rights would be specified in a contract. A range of databases and hard copy publications are designed to facilitate the choice of partners.[4] These provide an up-to-date review of the expertise available in British universities. Once a potential partner has been identified the industry liaison office at the university chosen would be the first point of contact.

Collaboration often takes place in science parks which can be found throughout the UK. Science parks have undergone considerable development in the last 20 years and several new parks are presently under construction. The UK hosts around 50 such parks – nearly one-third of the total for Europe. In the South East Trinity College, Cambridge developed the Ashford Science Park in Kent while Brunel University Park is located in Uxbridge. Other science parks in the South East include the Chilworth Research Centre in Southampton, Cranfield Technology Park, Oxford Science Park, South Bank Techno Park in London, Surrey Research Park (Guildford) and the University of Reading Innovation Centre.

Applied research and experimental development

Applied research and experimental development is often carried out within industry. Most R&D investment in the UK's manufacturing sector is concentrated in the pharmaceuticals (26 per cent), electrical machinery (18 per cent) and aerospace (13 per cent) sectors. While pharmaceuticals saw a significant real increase in R&D investment between 1990 and 1995 (+51 per cent), the electrical machinery (–21 per cent) and even more so the aerospace sector (–25 per cent) underwent a real

Table 4.5.1 *Regional expenditure on R&D performed in UK businesses by broad product groups*

	London	South East	South West	Eastern	East Midlands	West Midlands	Merseyside	Yorkshire and Humberside	North East	North West	Total UK
Manufacturing total	653	1,550	575	1,488	494	544	125	226	183	732	6,927
Chemicals	474	670	17	749	94	46	69	82	125	252	2,643
Mechanical engineering	16	151	28	174	38	66	4	38	31	51	659
Electrical machinery	109	316	209	139	(d)	116	(d)	12	14	73	1,234
Transport equipment	1	91	26	297	14	238	(d)	19	6	(d)	794
Aerospace	0	118	226	48	(d)	36	0	3	0	(d)	879
Other manufacturing	53	204	69	81	44	42	25	72	7	73	718
Services	226	748	201	537	123	120	2	54	47	260	2,452
Total	881	2,301	777	2,024	615	663	128	279	230	993	9,379

(d) denotes undisclosed figures.
Source: SET Statistics, 1997

decline in R&D expenditure.[5] The decline in the aerospace sector is largely a result of decreases in government funding for defence R&D. Regional expenditure on R&D by broad product group is presented in Table 4.5.1.

Regional distribution of funding

An analysis of the regional distribution of expenditure shows the South East being the most important region with 24.5 per cent of the UK total, followed by the Eastern region (21.6 per cent), the North West (10.6 per cent) and Greater London (9.4 per cent). Thus the South East and Greater London together attract more than one-third of all R&D expenditure in the UK. The chemical industry, including pharmaceuticals, accounts for almost 43 per cent of total UK R&D expenditure in the Greater London and the South East region – by far the most important R&D investor. It is followed by electrical machinery (34 per cent) and mechanical engineering (25 per cent). The aerospace industry undertakes 26 per cent of R&D expenditure in the South West (13 per cent in the South East) while the transport industry prefers the West Midlands, with almost 30 per cent of R&D expenditure undertaken in this region.

Within the chemical industry, the pharmaceutical sector plays the dominant role in the South East. The R&D scoreboard[6] shows that the top three spenders – Glaxo Wellcome, SmithKline Beecham and Zeneca (all pharmaceuticals) – together account for £2.5 billion, or almost 52 per cent of the R&D expenditure of the top ten R&D spenders in the UK. All three companies maintain R&D facilities in Greater London or the South East of England. Besides the strong commitment of the pharmaceuticals sector, the region has attracted the European R&D operations of large companies such as Hitachi in Berkshire, Fuji Copain in Kent, Nissan in Cranfield and Bull in Hertfordshire.

Science base

The Universities are largely responsible for the supply of young scientists. Two factors are believed to put supply side constraints on the output of young scientists in the UK. Problems of low status and hence low pay in engineering-related disciplines are said to discourage young people from obtaining a higher degree in this country. This has led to the problem of the 'brain-drain' – an outflow of young scientists (particularly to the USA) which was most pronounced between 1950 and 1970. Over the last 15 years governments have counteracted this by encouraging students to take up science and technology-related subjects – partly through an expansion of places in favour of science over arts and humanities. Today there is no evidence of a severe shortage of scientists or engineers. Home post-graduate output in engineering and technology has increased from 1,900 in 1988 to almost 3,400 in 1996. Computer science has seen a moderate increase from 1,500 to 1,690 postgraduates, with mathematics (from 290 to 620) and physics (from 1,960 to 2,894) showing the most dramatic increase between 1988 to 1996.[7] Undergraduate output follows a similar pattern over the same period. The number of engineering and technology graduates increased from 12,000 in 1988 to more than 18,000 in 1996.[8]

The most common complaint, however, particularly in the London area, concerns the relatively low pay for scientists in comparison to earnings in, for example, the accounting and legal professions. It is asserted that competition from the service sector crowds out industrial R&D in the labour market and many newly qualified scientists thus find work outside the scientific community. There is mixed evidence with regard to this hypothesis. The percentage of UK science, engineering and technology graduates actually working in science and technology is currently around 36 per cent for males and 21 per cent for females.[9] The majority of males qualified in the sciences, but working in non-science occupations, is concentrated in managerial positions (27 per cent) followed by other non-graduate positions (19 per cent). For women, other non-graduate positions account for 29 per cent, followed by teaching with 27 per cent. Although these figures indicate that apparent over-qualification is more marked for female graduates, only international comparison and observation over time will show whether this distribution is peculiar to Britain. Other data sources[10] show that the newly qualified engineer's and technologist's first choice is the manufacturing sector (29 per cent) with financial activities attracting a mere 2 per cent of new entrants.

Some factors are clearly easing supply side constraints in the South East. The local airport hub, feeder motorways, and the use of English have created a critical mass of R&D activity and hence personnel. People also enjoy working in the South East. There are good international schools, attractive greenfield sites, good employment opportunities for partners, low levels of personal taxation and close proximity to the capital.

R&D incentives

Britain's corporate tax rates are among the lowest in Europe. Additionally, investors may benefit, as we have suggested, from an average wage in some income groups less than half the level in continental Europe. Apart from schemes available on a European level[11] the British government offers incentives to promote R&D, some of them of distinct regional relevance. Small firms with fewer than 50 employees and a turnover smaller than £10 million can compete annually for grants paid out under the SMART (Small Firms Merit Award for Research and Technology) scheme. 'Regional Innovation' grants are available to firms with fewer than 50 employees for the development of innovative products undertaken in a number of areas in Britain, some of them in the South East and Greater London. The projects must incorporate a certain technical risk and degree of novelty of product and must lie above the normal R&D activities of the firm. SPUR (Support for Projects Under Research) sponsors the projects of firms (with fewer than 250 employees) which represent significant technological advance. All firms can benefit from the LINK scheme which aims to stimulate collaborative projects between research institutions and industry. The programme 'Club R&D' also encourages collaborative research, whereby a project is defined and companies are invited to contribute to the costs. The DTI will then cover up to 50 per cent of these costs.

Conclusion

Despite London's uneven educational performance at secondary level, standards of higher education in the capital are amongst the highest in the world. London's worldwide reputation as a vibrant, multicultural city further increase this skills base as highly skilled individuals from all over the world are drawn to the capital. Although this highly skilled workforce represents the largest concentration of labour in Europe, it is the deregulation of the previous 15 years that has given London a more significant competitive edge over other world cities. Increased atypical working, falling non-wage costs of employment, together with an increased use of competitive tendering from both the public and private sectors have helped reduce the costs of employment, allowing unemployment to fall at a rate not seen in the rest of Continental Europe.

As we move into the 21st century London's position as one of the most competitive global cities seems assured.

List of institutions set up to deal with London's skills base and other labour market issues

London First Centre

● Industry specific information on salary levels and other employee benefits;

- recommends specialist recruitment agencies and advisers;
- gives guidance on UK immigration law and work permits;
- provides information on training organisations and programmes;
- offers advice on souring multilingual staff including native language speakers.

Learning and Skills Council

- Training and development programmes for 16-24 year olds as well as recruitment advice for employers.
  Telephone 0207 896 8484
  Further information on the website: www.lsc.gov.uk

Oakland Consultancy
++44 1223 300 475 or http: //www.oakland.co.uk.

- Provides 'experts for industry' database on CD-ROM or floppy disc for an annual subscription. This contains 10,000 quality-assessed research topics funded by research councils and is searchable by researcher, institution and word search. Higher Education Funding Council research ratings also included;
- also provides a series of titles free of charge where universities promote their expertise and facilities in summary profile;
- Oaklands comprehensive survey of skills and expertise is available at http: www.cityscape.co.uk/oakland/dti/index/html.

Cartermill International
++44 1334 477 660

- Provides the 'BEST: Building Expertise in Science and Technology' database which records the qualifications of individual academics, their expertise, industrial experience, key patents and publications.

The London Chamber of Commerce and Industry provides a variety of services to members including information on the state of the London Economy. We are grateful for the access we have been given to this information as part of the joint project with the University of Westminster.

Notes

1 The Higher Education Funding Councils of England, Scotland and Wales (HEFCE, HEFCS and HEFCW) all follow the same procedure.
2 Examples include the *Medical Research Council* (MRC) and the *Science and Engineering Research Council* (SERC).

[3] For further information see, 'Research partnerships between industry and universities: a guide to better practice', which has been jointly prepared by the *Association for University Research, Industry Links* (AURIL) and the *Confederation of British Industry* (CBI), published in 1997 by CBI publications.

[4] See appendix.

[5] Figures taken from DTI (1997), *Science, Engineering and Technology Statistics 1997*, p 39.

[6] See Company Reporting (1997), *The UK R&D Scoreboard 1997*.

[7] ibid

[8] Op cit, p 45.

[9] See Glover *et al* (1996), 'What happens to women and men with SET degrees?', *Labour Market Trends*, February; pp 63–67.

[10] Higher Education Statistics Authority (HESA) (1997), *First Destinations of Students Leaving Higher Education Institutions 1994/95*, published in *DTI Science, Engineering and Technology Statistics*, p 54.

[11] The Department of Trade and Industry (DTI) may assist requests for funding under the European programmes COST, EUREKA and the wide range of European Framework programmes.

Part 5

Business Practice

5.1

UK International Tax Advantages

Geoff Collins,
BKR Haines Watts

This chapter focuses on the tax issues that an international company must address if it sets up business in London. The information given is necessarily general in nature. Since tax matters are inherently complex, professional advice should be sought in relation to specific situations or transactions.

Forms of business

An international company coming to London can choose two types of taxable presence: a branch or a subsidiary company.

UK branch of overseas parent company

Legally a branch is an extension of its parent company. This means that the financial results of the branch are consolidated with those of the parent company. Depending on the location of the parent company, they are generally included in the parent's own domestic corporate tax return. In the UK, the branch is nonetheless treated as if it were a stand-alone entity. It must file a corporation tax return with the Inland Revenue in respect of each accounting period. In assessing its taxable result, the branch must ensure that revenues and costs booked in its profit and loss account arising from transactions with the parent or other group entities are sustainable under the arm's length principle. We cover the arm's length principle later in this chapter.

Many branch operations make a trading loss in their first year or so as they invest in resources to gain a position in their particular marketplace. That loss may be available to set against any profits made by the parent in its domestic return, depending on the tax treatment of foreign branches under the domestic law of the parent company.

On the other hand, if the branch makes a profit, and pays UK corporation tax, the parent will normally be able to gain relief from double taxation on that profit in its own return under the terms of the relevant double taxation convention. In a number of countries the UK branch profits may be effectively exempted from further tax.

UK subsidiary company

A subsidiary company is an independent legal entity with its financial results taxed as such. As with a branch, the subsidiary must ensure that group costs and revenues comply with the arm's length principle.

If the subsidiary makes a trading loss in an accounting period, it has three options. It can elect to carry it back against taxable profits of the previous twelve months. It can elect to carry it forward to be used against future profits. Finally, it may be surrendered to other UK companies or branches in the same group.

If a UK subsidiary makes profits, it can declare a dividend payable to its parent company. Dividends are paid out of after tax profits. Although there is no withholding tax to be paid, the parent may obtain tax credit relief in its own jurisdiction in respect of UK underlying tax. Alternatively the dividend may be exempt from tax.

International taxation issues

The UK has the largest network of double taxation treaties in the world. It has treaties with all the major trading countries. The treaties are designed to avoid the double taxation of transactions. They give certainty to companies on how specific transactions and types of transactions will be taxed in each jurisdiction.

Putting an arm's length price on cross-border transactions between related companies is a fundamental requirement under UK tax. The UK follows the OECD transfer pricing guidelines in this respect. The arm's length price is the price that would have been agreed between the parties if they had been independent operators in possession of all relevant information. The OECD guidelines set out in detail acceptable methods for ascertaining such prices. In practical terms, it can be difficult to determine an arm's length price. One way of avoiding a future dispute with the Inland Revenue is to enter into an advance pricing agreement. This is possible where for example there is considerable difficulty in determining an appropriate method. Advance pricing agreements normally last for a period of three to five years and can involve the agreement of another tax authority (a bilateral agreement) or be a unilateral agreement with the UK Inland Revenue.

Assuming that no advance pricing agreement is in force, and a dispute arises with the Revenue, who consider an adjustment necessary, the way forward is either to apply the mutual agreement procedure under the respective double taxation treaty or to use the EU Arbitration Convention adopted by the UK in 1995.

Thin capitalisation

One important aspect of the arm's length principle concerns overseas companies financing UK operations through debt. They need to ask whether a third party such as a bank would make a loan of such an amount, and whether the rate of interest charged on the principal is in line with market rates, considering the risk involved. If any interest is charged that goes beyond what is commercially reasonable, then the Inland Revenue may disallow it as an expense for corporation tax.

Corporation tax returns and the payment of tax

Every taxable corporate entity must file a self-assessment corporation tax return (CT600) within twelve months of the end of its accounting period. If the accounting period is longer than twelve months, it is divided into two periods of account for corporation tax purposes: the first period is twelve months since the last period, and the second the remaining period. It must file both corporation tax returns within twelve months of the end of its long accounting period.

Corporation tax returns filed late are subject to an automatic fine of £100. If there is a further delay of three months or more there is a further fine of £100. After a delay of 18 months, tax-geared penalties apply.

For corporate entities with profits below the large company threshold of £1.5 million, corporation tax is due within nine months the end of each accounting period.

Once its profits exceed the large company threshold, the company will be required to settle its corporation tax liability by means of four payments on account. The first two are in months seven and ten of the current accounting period. The final two are in months one and four of the following accounting period. Because the first two payments on account, and possibly the remaining two as well, have to be made before the results of the accounting period are known, it is important for the entity to estimate its results as accurately as possible. If the tax paid is less than it should have been, the Inland Revenue was charged interest on late payment.

Conversely, if the entity overpays, the Inland Revenue will pay interest. In either case, the interest will be brought into the entity's accounts as taxable income or tax deductible expense.

It should be mentioned that there are special provisions covering entities entering the payments on account regime for the first time. In addition, for entities already in the charge to corporation tax, there is a transitional regime ending in 2002.

Corporation tax rates

The financial year for corporation tax in the UK runs from 1 April to 31 March in the following year. Corporation tax rates are set annually in the Finance Act that is usually enacted in the summer of the financial year concerned. The rates are however announced before the start of the financial year in the annual budget announcement in March.

The rates applying in the 2000 – 2001 financial year are:

Level of profits	Rate
£1 – £10,000	10%
£10,001 – £50,000	20% less marginal relief
£50,001 – £350,000	20%
£350,001 – £1,500,000	30% less marginal relief
£1,500,001 –	30%

Marginal relief has the effect of reducing the rate on total profits to a proportionate rate falling between the higher and lower rate.

Where a UK company is part of a group, the thresholds in the above table are reduced pro rata for each trading member of the group. Thus a company belonging to a simple group, consisting of two trading companies, will pay 30 per cent tax once its profits reach £750,000.

Calculating taxable profits

The starting point for calculating the taxable profit of a UK company is the profit shown in the profit and loss account for statutory reporting purposes, determined in accordance with the UK's generally accepted accounting principles (GAAP). The statutory profit is then adjusted for changes required under UK tax law. In past times, the number of these adjustments was extensive. However over the last few years the Inland Revenue have moved more and more in the direction of accepting an entity's statutory profits drawn up under GAAP without the need for change.

Some adjustments that are still needed include the following:

- accounting depreciation of fixed assets is not allowed against tax. Instead there is a system of capital allowances in respect of specified categories of fixed assets;
- entertaining and hospitality expenditure is not allowed for tax purposes;
- expenditure of a capital nature is not allowed against trading profits. An example of such expenditure is the legal expense of obtaining a lease on premises;
- dividends are not an expense against profits. They are instead a distribution of after tax profits. As already noted, interest on inter-company financing from overseas in excess of a reasonable commercial rate is also treated as a distribution.

The UK has a schedular system of tax. This means that different categories of income are taxed under different schedules. For companies, the main schedules are A and D. Schedule A covers property income whereas schedule D is divided into a number of sub-schedules called cases. Trading income falls into case I, interest income into case III, and sundry other income into case VI. The main purpose of the schedular system has been to stop profits taxed under one schedule being reduced by losses in another. However, with the availability of loss relief against total income from both trading and rental income, the schedular system has lost much of its validity, and is considered by many commentators to be outdated. Nonetheless, some restrictions survive. For example, a trading loss cannot be carried forward against future interest income.

Specific tax incentives for UK entities

The UK Government has introduced, or is consulting on, a number of important tax incentives for companies. These will be of interest to international companies considering the UK as a business location. They include:

First year capital allowances on equipment and machinery

Small companies may write off, in the year of purchase, 100 per cent of any expenditure on capital equipment that is information technology related. This includes computers, computer peripherals and data equipment, third general mobile telephones and software. The criteria for a small company, two of which must be met, are employees not more than 50, sales revenues not more than £2.8 million and balance sheet total not more than £1.4 million.

Medium-sized companies can claim a 40 per cent write-off on the same items. Both small and medium-sized companies may claim a first year capital allowance of 40 per cent against profits on expenditure on any many other categories of plant and machinery used for the purpose of their business. The criteria for a medium-sized company, two of which must be met, are employees not more than 250, sales revenues not more than £11.2 million and balance sheet total not more than £5.6 million.

Research and development tax credits

Small or medium-sized companies investing in research and development activities in the UK are allowed to offset 150 per cent of the related costs against future profits.

Corporate venturing relief

Trading companies meeting the relevant criteria who make strategic minority investments in other stand-alone companies undertaking qualifying trading activities, are allowed to write the cost of those investments off against tax in the period in which they are made.

Disposals of substantial shareholdings

Under current law, a UK company disposing of its shareholding in a subsidiary or associated company is taxed on any gain arising. The Government is consulting on providing relief against such tax, either by means of a deferral of the gain if rolled into a new substantial shareholding, or by means of tax exemption altogether. The outcome of the Government's deliberations is likely to feature in the 2001 Finance Act.

Tax relief on intellectual property costs

The Government proposes to extend corporation tax reliefs on the acquisition and development of intangible assets. At present these are exceedingly modest, with companies obtaining no tax relief at all unless the intangible asset is subsequently disposed of. The main thrust of the Government's proposals is to move to allow expense to be allowed for corporation tax to the extent it is reported in the company's profit and loss account under UK GAAP. Again, the outcome of the Government's deliberations is likely to feature in the 2001 Finance Act.

London as a location for a European headquarters holding company

London has always been a popular choice for setting up a European headquarters holding company. Many factors such as the English language, the existence of a skilled workforce, the UK's flexible labour market and the pre-eminence of London as an international financial centre make a compelling case in the minds of overseas companies wishing to exploit the European marketplace. From a tax perspective, the proposition was also an attractive one since the UK has relatively low headline rates of corporate income tax as well as low employment taxes.

One problem with setting up headquarters in the UK was that dividends received from foreign subsidiaries were taxed again when received in the UK. UK tax legislation gave some relief, by allowing foreign tax paid to be credited against the holding company's UK corporation tax, but only up to the extent of the UK tax. If the foreign tax paid was greater than the UK tax, then the holding company could not get relief for all the foreign tax. To get round this problem, the holding company could channel dividends from European subsidiaries through offshore structures that evened out, or mixed, the high and low taxes in foreign jurisdictions. In the Finance Act 2000, the Government enacted legislation to restrict this offshore pooling of dividends from overseas subsidiaries. The new rules, the details of which remain to be finalised in 2001, are due to come into force on 1 April 2001. They will restrict credit relief on dividends to those subject to an underlying tax rate of 45 per cent.

Share incentives

The UK has a number of tax privileged share arrangements designed to incentivise either all employees generally or specific groups such as senior executives. These include the all employee share ownership trust and the enterprise management incentive scheme. Both arrangements were launched in 2000 as replacements for previous schemes. Essentially these schemes defer tax on the employee until the eventual sale of his or her shares. They also exempt the employer from national insurance which would otherwise be chargeable.

The UK's tax-driven share schemes are generally not suited to the branches or subsidiaries of overseas companies. The UK operations will usually wish to motivate and reward local UK management with membership of the parent company's share or option arrangements in the overseas jurisdiction. As a result, the employees and the employer may suffer unexpected tax and national insurance consequences. They should seek professional advice in the structuring of local benefit packages. One recent legislative change in the UK has enabled employers to transfer their own national insurance burden onto the employee, subject to the employee's advance agreement at the time of option grant. Whether employees are prepared to accept the resulting 52 per cent marginal tax rate is of course a different matter.

Relocation costs

The costs of relocating employees and their families into the UK are fully tax deductible for the UK branch or company incurring the cost. Relocation costs are treated as income of the employee concerned and subject to income tax. However there is an exemption for eligible relocation costs under the limit of £8000. In addition, there is special tax relief for the travelling expenses of the expatriate foreign employee and his or her family in visiting or coming to the UK.

UK property taxes

UK businesses occupying commercial property pay a property tax called the uniform business rate to the local government authority in the area. In London the local authorities are the Corporation of London in City of London and the individual London boroughs outside the City.

The uniform business rate is a percentage that is applied to the rateable value. It is a national multiplier set annually by the Government. To arrive at the rateable value, the Government's surveyors have to assess the property's potential rentable value. It has no connection with the business actually carried out on the property. For advice on the uniform business rate as it applies to any particular property, businesses should consult a suitably qualified property adviser such as a chartered surveyor.

Stamp duty

Stamp duty is levied on the execution of certain legal documents. The principal documents affected are share purchases and land transactions.

Stamp duty is charged on share transactions at the rate of 0.5 per cent. Since many overseas jurisdictions have no such duty, the levying of stamp duty makes the UK uncompetitive. As long ago as 1991, with the motive of protecting the important securities industry in the City of London, the Government enacted legislation to abolish stamp duty on share transactions from a day to be appointed in the future. Unfortunately the Government has never gone ahead with setting the appointed day.

The rate of stamp duty on property transactions has steadily increased in recent years. The current maximum rate is 4 per cent applying to property transactions over £500,000 in value. Since properties in the London area are worth more than comparable ones in the provinces, it follows that companies setting up business in London should budget for stamp duty as a significant extra cost. This cost will be borne when they take on commercial premises. It is also to be taken into account if they relocate employees into the London area, since their relocation packages will have to cover stamp duty on the purchase of a home in London. In some cases, stamp duty alone will exceed the £8000 tax free limit referred to above.

VAT

VAT is a European tax. UK registered companies are required to charge VAT on taxable supplies of goods and services in accordance with UK tax law which implements the EU's Sixth VAT Directive. For many companies VAT is straightforward. In their quarterly VAT returns, they calculate the VAT on sales made and deduct from it VAT paid on purchases. They then declare and pay over the net amount to H M Customs and Excise.

Companies making a mixture of exempt and taxable supplies face a number of difficulties. One is to agree a basis on which non-attributable input tax can be reasonably allocated to taxable and exempt supplies. Another is to determine which supplies are exempt in the first place and which are not. In the financial sector, which predominates in the City of London, lack of clarity in the governing legislation has led to many VAT disputes. These have principally concerned the VAT treatment of services that are ancillary to exempt financial and insurance services.

Another major problem with VAT is the treatment of cross-border services. There is a complicated matrix of rules for determining the place of supply of services. Factors to be taken into account include the commercial status of the recipient of the service, the country in which the supplier is based, the country in which the recipient is based, and the intrinsic nature of the service itself by reference to the provisions of the Sixth VAT Directive.

The UK has always sought to implement the provisions of the Sixth VAT Directive in a way that reduces the compliance burdens on business. However this has in several instances backfired on H M Customs. They have been forced into anti-avoidance procedures that actually increase compliance burdens. A classic example of this is the facilitation measure that allows companies in the same group to elect for group VAT treatment. This allows them to report all their VAT-related transactions on a single VAT return and to dispense with the charging of VAT between group members. Inevitably many companies, particularly in the exempt sector, have put in place structures that fall within the group treatment rules that result in considerable tax savings. In an attempt to counteract these structures, H M Customs have instigated a succession of legislative changes. They have given themselves wide-ranging powers to nullify group structures on the grounds of the protection of the revenue. The upshot is that a measure that was meant to help companies has become something of a minefield requiring expert professional advice.

The European Commission is well aware of the problems of the complexity of VAT, particularly in relation to cross-border transactions and the exempt sector. They have proposed a radical overhaul of the entire system, but have not made any significant headway in persuading the member states to adopt it.

Part 6

The City of London

6.1

Keeping an Eye on Brussels

John Houston,
Houston Consulting Europe

'Oh no! Not another regulation from Brussels! Who do these people talk to? Why wasn't I told?!'

Things have come some way since the days when this was the standard City response to most developments in Brussels affecting the financial services sector. But it is still too widespread a reaction for comfort. And similar reactions were heard publicly recently after the European Commission published draft directives on market manipulation and on prospectuses. Many City experts held that the latter in particular, as proposed, threatened the future of important segments of City business.

Why does there still seem to be so often this clash between the City and 'Brussels'? Is it simply a failure of communication? Is it more profound: a clash of cultures between a freewheeling and entrepreneurial City, and an institutional system in Brussels prone to regulation? Is it even part of a plot by competitor financial centres to hamstring the City and gain time to build up competitive capacity? Or does it have an entirely different explanation?

Bridges to Brussels

Before looking at these questions, I would first suggest that the problem itself tends to be much exaggerated. There is a huge flow of co-operation, consultation and dialogue between the City and Brussels every day. This has many components, including the 'intermediary' work of HMT and the FSA, following a constant stream of local consultations; the advocacy and communication work of the

Corporation of London, bringing MEPs to the City, visiting Brussels, publishing research; the constant stream of travellers to Brussels from City trade associations and financial services firms; and the work of Brussels-based consultants.

Trade associations have made enormous strides in recent years in building co-ordinated efforts, with many of them tending by informal agreement to take the lead on an issue, and the others rowing in behind to lend support. Some of these organizations have developed pan-European reach, or reinforced their role in the relevant EU level federation. Position papers supported by Brussels-based financial services organisations sometimes have their origin in a trade body or other organisation based in the City. It was a mixture of City and Brussels-based trade associations, together with some big financial institutions from various EU member states including the UK, which originated an effort to establish communication exchanges with MEPs, now carried out via the rather successful European Parliamentary Financial Services Forum.

Individual firms, or *ad hoc* groupings of such firms, also play a major part in the Brussels policy process. Most of the major players in the City, and in other EU financial markets, have high-powered specialists in EU and regulatory affairs, who either travel regularly to Brussels to brief EU officials or are actually based there.

Brussels-based EU affairs consultants, some of whom specialise in financial sector issues, play an important role in supplying the financial industry with the necessary information and intelligence on EU developments. They also supply analysis, advice, strategic and tactical counselling, and practical support on the ground, such as for management of events. They provide a pool of skilled multinational, and frequently multilingual, people which can be flexibly tapped into by institutions to augment their resources. Although there seems only to be one specialist financial services boutique operation in Brussels offering the whole range of such services, most of the big communications groups have some capability in the sector.

So the voice of the City is far from silent, and the gap between it and Brussels certainly has a large number of bridges across it. But the communication is still apparently difficult. There remains mutual misunderstanding, erroneous or over-simplified expectations, and consequently frustration and distrust.

New Developments on Consultation

More systematic and fuller consultation and transparency can and will help to address such difficulties. This is very much on the EU agenda today, following the famous report by the group of 'wise men' headed by Baron Lamfalussy. The Lamfalussy Report recommended, and the EU institutions are now in the process of implementing, an approach to the EU legislative and policy process which was much more transparent and open to input from experts and interested parties. Lamfalussy in particular laid stress on the importance of pre-consultation – rather than the presentation of pre-cooked texts for comment – and further dialogue at all stages.

This should allow the utility of any measures, as well as their general shape and detail, to be tested thoroughly against market realities and the best available expertise.

The practice of EU institutions has heretofore been at best erratic – the existence and extent of consultation has too often depended on the mood or inclination of the responsible officials, the perceived need for speed, and the willingness of individual member states to conduct domestic consultations on the issues. The idea that better consultation and more transparency usually means better legislation – and often more speed in the legislative process itself – is a relatively new one on many quarters. This is true not only of parts of the 'Brussels' machine, but to an even greater extent of many national authorities.

The Lamfalussy group crystallised a new mood and a moment of change on these practices. Hopefully, it has also been the catalyst for a qualitative step-change, where firm rules on consultation and transparency are hard-wired into the system. This should be a process of continuous mutual engagement in which the financial services industry will play its proper part.

Culture Clash

But what of the supposed culture clash between entrepreneurial markets and the 'dead hand of bureaucracy' in Brussels?

We should first remember that 'Brussels' – in the form of the European Commission – has often been the main source of an impetus for open and competitive European markets. EU governments have frequently had to be dragged kicking and screaming into the 21st century when it came to competition in telecommunications, airlines, energy and numerous other industries. Successive European Commissions, and in particular the Competition, Industry and Internal Market Commissioners, have harried and prodded reluctant national authorities towards the kind of cross-border competition which has given Europe, in some areas, world-beating industries – and could do so in others in the future.

The notion of a heavy-handed bureaucracy in Brussels keen to regulate everything which moves, in contrast to the fair and reasonable regulation from friendly national authorities, is very far from reality.

Nonetheless, EU processes do inevitably reflect the fact of different reflexes around Europe as to what should and should not be regulated, and how. The consequences have sometimes been problematic: over-prescriptive and excessively detailed legislation; a tendency to regulate yesterday's developments rather than to address those of tomorrow; and, a particularly common fault – messy, ambiguous compromises on matters where member states were deeply divided. All of these and more have led to complaints from the private sector, including in the City, that EU regulation is more likely to be a general handicap than a spur to cross-border business.

There are cultural elements to the underlying causes of these problems, including an interpretation in some member states of independence which has bred arrogance – and sometimes ignorance – among government officials; rule and law-making processes which do not provide for flexible application, nor for speedy adaptation and updating; a tendency in some quarters to see law as declaratory, rather than needing to be applied in detail, and so on.

Some regulators have traditionally taken the view that independence required them to have limited contact with those subject to regulation and supervision. The view was that the authorities had a duty to the public whose requirements they understood (by some undefined process of osmosis) better than special interests. One still hears similar sentiments today, but generally speaking times have changed, or are changing. Most officials across Europe now understand that neither the public interest, nor effective regulation, can be defined in a vacuum.

Concerns about excessively rigid and over-prescriptive legislation are often coupled with complaints about ambiguity and legislative overlap regarding cross-border rights under EU law. There is a certain ambivalence here on the part of business – on the one hand seeking certainty about details of cross-border rights, and on the other wanting flexible legislation which does not over-prescribe, particularly on matters where the speed of market or technological innovation is liable to make rules quickly out of date. Related complaints about lack of a level playing field, about the other fellow not playing by the rules (the concern is not confined to the UK), also underline the need to build a coherent common culture of enforcement and compliance.

Fortunately this is what is already under way in the securities segment at least. The legislative and rule-making structure flowing from the Lamfalussy Report should create a degree of convergence among both regulators and supervisors, which will tackle many of the cultural obstacles to market-opening legislation. It involves framework legislation, establishing the agreed principles; a secondary legislation process via a Securities Committee, which can provide for quick updating e.g. on technical matters; and a Committee of European Securities Regulators (CESR – now becoming commonly known as Caesar), through which European securities supervisors will in common develop both detailed recommendations for the legislation at the above two levels, and agree detailed standards for implementation. In addition the European Commission retains its duty of enforcement before the European Court when necessary.

This process is no cure-all. But it offers a better prospect of satisfactory regulatory frameworks for European securities markets than anything else to date. If it works it is likely to influence the way other financial sector rules are approached.

National competition

Of course competition between national financial centres, and lobbying by less competitive companies for protection, form an important backdrop to all of this. Member states do seek national advantage in the policy and legislative process, and City interests do not always come out on top.

Some members states have dragged their feet in opening up their markets, whether as an automatic reflex, sheer chauvinism and narrow-mindedness, or as a result of calculated promotion of some domestic interest. Sometimes there is no obvious policy control – it is not necessary to look very far to identify a European state where the political leadership is firmly committed to open competition across borders, while the financial services bureaucracy carries on regardless with traditional policies which are illiberal and protectionist.

So it is not always a case of Machiavellian plots or calculated obstruction. The 'cock-up' and conspiracy theories of history both have their place, together with simple bad habits and the dead weight of the status quo.

All of these are challenged by the new processes being put in place. Peer pressure, working through details of practice together at all levels, agreed targets and benchmarks – these are bricks in the construction now being erected to make integration of Europe's financial markets work. There is reason to believe they will make a difference, even if not as quickly or as dramatically as many of us would like.

Conclusion

EU leaders and all EU institutions have firmly committed themselves to implementation of the 'Financial Services Action Plan' within the next four years. To make this possible they have set up structures for accelerated decision-making, technical updates via secondary processes, and intensive collaborative efforts between Europe's regulators and supervisors.

This action plan contains a mix of measures, 43 in all, which are intended to have a general effect of liberalising cross-border competition and integrating markets. But this comes with a price tag, in the form of balancing measures to tighten supervisory, prudential, and consumer protection rules. And the liberalising measures could be weakened unless strong pressure is maintained to ensure the full upside is realised.

City interests have a strong voice in this process. But so too, and quite properly, do interests from many other parts of the EU. The difference for the City is the concentration of expertise and international firms which it can bring to bear on the issues. With the new, more thorough, consultative processes in place, the necessary commitment and effort on the part of City players can help to ensure measurable progress in making EU financial markets more open and globally competitive by the year 2004.

6.2

The City of London – Global Centre for European Finance

Judith Mayhew,
Corporation of London

The City of London has been an important trading centre since Roman times and the world's pre-eminent international trading centre since the beginning of the seventeenth century. Today, at the onset of the twenty-first century, the City of London, at the heart of the Greater London metropolis, is the world's leading international financial and business centre and by far the largest financial centre in Europe.

Physically, the City of London is tightly packed; most of its international business houses are situated within a 2.8 square kilometre area, with a large proportion of the remainder sitting within a 2 kilometre radius. The square mile constitutes the greatest collection of international, wholesale and specialist retail financial markets in one location within Europe.

Its 478 overseas banks transact 19 per cent of world cross border lending;

One third of global foreign exchange turnover is executed in London, compared to 18 per cent in New York, 5 per cent in Frankfurt and 3.6 per cent in Paris. The main currencies traded are the dollar with 33 per cent of business; and the Euro at 29 per cent. Sterling is only 8 per cent.

The City is also the world's largest derivative centre with 36 per cent of over the counter business and an almost complete domination (over 95 per cent) of Euro short-term interest rate derivatives.

The London Stock Exchange trades 58 per cent of foreign equity turnover. Euro denominated stocks now comprise the largest sector by currency and the capitalisation of stocks on the London Stock Exchange is nearly double that of both Frankfurt or Paris;

And lastly the City is the largest centre for institutional fund management with nearly $2.5 trillion under management.

Key to the success of the City are its openness and attraction to foreign businesses – over 65 per cent of the Fortune Global 500 companies, in all sectors, not just finance, are now represented in London. European Union business is particularly important with the number of EU-based banks growing from 100 in 1995 to 108 in 1999, employing over 30,000 staff and having some $1.5 trillion in assets. It is therefore hardly surprising that a significant proportion of London's business is denominated in euros. For instance, 66 per cent of international equities; 72 per cent of derivatives; and 29 per cent of foreign exchange are traded in that currency.

In addition to involvement in pure banking, these organisations all have large departments in corporate finance, securities and derivatives. Furthermore many of these international houses have now centralised their international treasury and risk management in the City and often euro foreign exchange, international bond and equity trading, and research are also based in London. Non-government euro bond and equity insurance and M & A advisory business are mainly centred in London as well, alongside the very considerable operations of the American banks who maintain a large presence here.

All this allows business operating here to enjoy substantial economies of scale and scope as a result of the presence of the full range of financial and professional services operating in one location. The EU derives enormous benefit from this concentration. The EU further profits from the City's global span and its huge multinational base; as well as its large volumes of trade. These, in turn, allow the provision of a range of financial services on a level that makes them incredibly cost effective.

Meanwhile the strength and depth of London's markets has created a liquidity that enables competitive pricing for transactions of all sizes and for non-standard products. The City is truly the meeting place of the dollar, the Yen and the Euro. Recent studies have clearly demonstrated that if such a concentration of services were not provided in London, some 52 per cent of business would either not be economic or would emigrate to centres outside the EU[1]. The same studies illustrate that if these services were ever to be fragmented for any reason, EU customers would undoubtedly suffer from unwelcome increased costs. The City of London is therefore a crucial component of the whole EU economy, it boosts its efficiency and its competitiveness – and hence Europe's GDP.

So why has London been more successful than other financial centres in attracting this international business?

The Corporation of London commissioned studies to examine the needs of the City in the future where London was compared with New York. Remarkable similarities were observed both in their economies and in their ability to attract young, mobile, international workers in finance and advanced business services.

For many of these people, London is seen as 'the place to be'. London is an excellent place in which to live and work and the population has increased by over four per cent in the last ten years. Whilst, of course, some of this has been due to standard immigration, a significant proportion is attributable to the generation of new jobs for skilled professionals, the talented and the creative. London is the place with the best market infrastructure and largest pool of researchers, traders, brokers, lawyers, regulators, IT specialists and investment managers which make up the market. They are the people who derive business value by their skills and their innovation. The moves of these highly skilled professionals from other economies to London can be directly linked to the development and expansion of financial related business. A large number of their jobs have been created by the considerable levels of inward investment pouring into London. Moreover the companies that generate inward investment are commonly innovative and vigorous. They contribute strongly to both current and future prosperity and their presence in tandem with the largest financial institutions in the world engenders enormous competitiveness that, in turn, increases efficiency and lowers costs.

Financial and business services executives enjoy coming to London, both to work and to live. Financial practitioners are well paid and they work hard.

But they, and their families, do expect to live a comfortable life style with access to quality houses and schools, good restaurants and shopping, including a variety of Japanese shops and restaurants, as well as a fine array of arts and culture.

The tax and legal regime is also central to the success of a financial centre. In Britain, businesses and individuals are offered the benefits of a benign tax regime and a tax efficient location when compared to many centres in continental Europe. Social security taxes are also considerably lower.

Also a number of measures introduced in recent years have increased tax benefits to companies, particularly international holding companies. Add to this a relatively predictable and sensible legal system and you produce a marked competitive advantage for London.

As with all international centres, London's businessmen need to undertake frequent journeys to a wide range of destinations and we are fortunate in that there are five easily accessible international airports. Over 250 destinations are served by a direct flight at least once a week. London–New York is the world's busiest long haul route and London–Paris the busiest short haul route.

We calculate that around 40 per cent of the great army of people employed in the City now work for non-British employers. We are no longer simply a British financial services centre, we have become a financial centre that belongs to the entire world.

Such talent undoubtedly adds to London's other unique selling points – its embrace of technology, telecommunications and the associated software industry. Britain has the most open telecommunications environment in Europe, with 150 operators licensed to provide services, with 40 of them in the City where there are 12 fibre optic ring mains to cope with the technological demand. London is also a major centre for information technology and software. London teleport, the world's largest satellite earth station, provides links for an average 2500 outside broadcasts each month. The London Internet exchange is the world's largest Internet hub and the transit point for much of Europe's Internet traffic.

London is also home to the new breed of backbone operators with state of the art high capacity fibre optic networks linking major cities across Europe. Over the last twelve months a tremendous amount of new transmission capacity, or bandwidth, has been added to these links, and this extra capacity has led to staggering price declines. For instance a transatlantic circuit that could be leased for 15 years in 1997 for $16 million is now priced at only $850,000 for the same period and prices are continuing to fall to the tune of some 50–60 per cent a year.

The presence of the financial services industry in the City has enabled London to become one of the top three elite world financial software industry centres – the other two being New York and Chicago, with 61,000 people being employed in computer and related industries.

In addition, London is also a centre for financial innovation in derivatives. European and US companies in this industry are clustered in London and they contribute towards the highly sophisticated leveraged trading and risk management strategies used in these products, thereby further increasing linkage of finance and information technology.

This technological centre is supported by a unique knowledge base within London's universities. Imperial College, University College London, Queen Mary and Westfield College and City University provide telecommunication and IT expertise that is unsurpassed in the world.

The final key to London's success is the presence of a vibrant property market with a large supply of international investors and developers. Very high quality property from an investment perspective as well as provision of modern, flexible office buildings are very important factors in the retention of international firms in London. In the City during the early 1990s, 250,000 square feet was the norm for the largest institutions office requirements. Today 750,000 to 1 million square feet is required. International financial institutions are prime players and by necessity they bring a long-term commitment to flexible buildings, capable of keeping up to date with the ever-increasing sophistication of IT and telecommunications, allowing for the continuous renewal of office stock to the latest technical and environmental standards.

This conglomeration of successful businesses in combination with a high quality international workforce has enabled London to remain at the forefront of change and innovation in Europe's capital markets and in the development of the euro. A major proportion of currency expertise in Europe is resident in the City and they are producing new ideas; this is triggering market changes. These changes are reflected in the future outlook.

The electronic market place is now allowing financial traders and brokers such a global reach that it is far easier for them to trade from a single location. Add to this the requirement for professional and well-informed people to surround markets and provide the necessary skill and added value. In the City of London that very asset exists in abundance. London's dominance in foreign exchange, derivatives, cross-border bank lending and euro-denominated international bond markets mean that it is continuing to clearly outpace Frankfurt and Paris as an international financial centre. Deep and liquid euro markets have become well-established in London, replacing the more segmented markets in the old national currencies such as the Deutschemark. London now accounts for more than half of the issues of euro-denominated international bonds and 70 per cent of secondary trading in the market. London additionally accounts for 19 per cent of cross-border flows in Target, the European payments system, up from 15 per cent when the euro was launched.

However the European financial services market is still too fragmented. A significant number of barriers for financial services within Europe persist and the single market in financial services is certainly far from complete. Baron Alexandre Lamfalussy, who chaired the committee of 'wise men', describes the current position as 'a remarkable cocktail of Kafkaesque inefficiency that serves no one'. The committee has suggested adoption of common accounting rules, easier and cheaper cross-border clearing and settlement, reform of the rules for issuing prospectuses and gaining stock market listings. These are to be welcomed. However, the City operates in a rapidly changing environment and the only certainty is that the markets in 2004, the end of the Lamfalussy timetable, will look different to how they look now. There is a danger that we may still be attempting to sort out common standards for the markets based on how they appear today.

In the final analysis, everything else that we do is based around our success in the competitive international market place. For any market, part of the attraction is the right degree of regulation with the requirements that are laid on it being sufficient to give confidence to its participants without pressing down on them. We are fortunate as the FSA provides such a framework.

People have confidence that the square mile is the place where business is properly regulated, fair and certain. Above all the City of London is the place where world-class business works, and world-class businessmen want to be.

Notes

[1] *The City's importance to the EU economy.* Centre for Economic and Business Research November 2000

6.3

The City of London – Bank of England

Peter Rodgers for Sir Edward George,
Bank of England

When the first edition of 'London as an International Business Centre' was published in 1998, the launch of the euro was just a few months away. I was confident that the City would be prepared, and it was. London was ready to offer euro-denominated financial services from the start of the new year's business on 4 January 1999. Part of London's readiness was down to the considerable efforts across the City – in which the Bank played a co-ordinating role – to ensure that the necessary systems had been put in place and tested. But it was also due to the City's long experience and expertise in conducting international business.

At the time of the euro's launch, it was occasionally suggested that business might drift away from London to the Continent, since the UK had not joined the single currency itself. However, financial activity thrives wherever it can be pursued conveniently, efficiently and profitably. Seen in these terms, the advent of the euro has been an opportunity, not a threat. It has provided London with the chance to consolidate its position as the leading European international financial centre and to develop new euro-denominated [or euro-related] financial markets. For example, around a third of total daily turnover in foreign exchange is traded in London. London also has a market share of around 55 per cent of underwritten euro-denominated Eurobond issuance and an estimated 70 per cent of secondary trading in the Eurobond market. Almost 40 per cent of equity trades reported to the London Stock Exchange are denominated in euro.

Looking ahead, the Government has announced that, within two years of the general election, it will assess against five economic tests whether going into EMU would be in the national interest. Its policy is to prepare and decide. In terms of the practical preparations required for possible UK entry, the Bank is playing a key role in the financial sector including drawing lessons from the experience of euro area countries preparing for the introduction of notes and coin at the beginning of 2002.

The other major development anticipated in the first edition of this book, which has since become a reality, is the adoption of the Financial Services and Markets Act. The Financial Services Authority has now taken the place of nine previous regulatory bodies. Under the old system, the cost of regulation was becoming a key concern for the financial services industry. The creation of a single regulator has helped to increase the efficiency of the system. It has also helped provide a more complete and accurate picture of large financial conglomerates. Consolidation of financial firms has been accelerating in recent years, as documented by the recent G10 report on financial sector consolidation, as firms seek to diversify risks and provide global services to global customers. Consolidation has featured prominently in the UK. It is estimated that almost a third of the total value of domestic banking mergers in the EU during the 1990s is accounted for by the UK.

The process of consolidation has also been increasingly evident in the financial infrastructure – trading, clearing, payment and settlement systems. While the market for trading systems is contestable, as witnessed by the intensification of competition between trading platforms in recent years, clearing, payment and settlement systems – the plumbing that runs through financial markets – are closer to natural monopolies. With the continued development of new technology, settlement cycles are shortening, clearing houses are expanding the range of products they can handle, and work is under way to eliminate intra-day credit exposures in the settlement of credit exposures.

In all these areas – the development of euro-denominated markets, the transformation of the financial regulatory and supervisory regime, and the ability to adopt and develop new technologies to improve conditions for business – London continues to demonstrate its dynamism and ability to spot, identify and seize opportunities. These have always been valuable attributes and will continue to be as we enter into the 21st century and a more integrated, competitive global economy.

Part 7

Business Support and Information

7.1

VC Provision

Ali Erfan,
3i

Background

Venture capital was formally added to London's range of financial skills during the 1980s, although it had existed, in fact if not in name, before that. Its impact on the British economy has been immense. It has backed new enterprises which could not have emerged otherwise, and existing companies have been helped to grow in a way which would have been impossible if they had had to rely entirely on overdraft finance. Venture capital transactions have also facilitated large-scale corporate restructuring, by making it possible for large organisations to divide into smaller, more efficient units.

Until 20 years ago venture capital was largely thought of in the UK as being American and slightly alien. The need for a UK equivalent had been spelled out as far back as the early 1930s, when an official body, the Macmillan Committee, identified a gap in the financial markets: while large companies could obtain equity capital by going to the stock market, Macmillan noted that smaller companies had difficulty in finding long-term backing.

Nothing was really done to fill the 'Macmillan Gap' until the closing months of World War II when, in line with the national determination that there must be no return to the pre-war depression, the Bank of England and the clearing banks set up a company to provide long-term capital to enable small and medium-sized companies to grow. That company, which has been active in backing business growth since 1945, is now known as 3i.[1]

The early 1980s saw a number of dramatic developments. Partly it was the growing impact of global competition, but much of the change was political. The Thatcher Government believed in an 'enterprise culture' to encourage enterprising individuals to set up in business, while harsh financial disciplines drove inefficient businesses to the wall.

The 'enterprise revolution' attracted large sums of capital from British and international sources to back a new breed of entrepreneurs – often people who in the past would have climbed up the hierarchy of a big corporation but in the new climate chose the exciting option of running their own company.

The British Venture Capital Association was established as a voice of the new industry which grew up to back such people.

During the 1990s the London venture market further developed its techniques for profitable investment in the UK, and increasingly also looked for opportunities in continental Europe. According to the 3i/PricewaterhouseCoopers Global Private Equity 2001 report, $12.2 bn of private equity and venture capital was invested in the UK in 2000.

Venture capital products

Venture capital is applicable in a range of business situations. Various financial instruments are available, of which the most important is equity, share capital, subscribed partly by the managers of the business and partly by their backers. This may be supported with some form of preference shares and with loan capital.

What all venture-backed situations have in common is that the managers are determined to make the business grow, potentially providing significant rewards both to them and to the supplier and of the venture capital.

Start-ups and emerging businesses

These businesses will have been founded by people with appropriate experience and an impressive track record, plus entrepreneurial qualities. They will have identified a market opportunity where they will have competitive advantage in providing products or services in strong demand.

Backers always expect the founders of a company to be willing to invest an appropriate amount of their own money. They recognise that young business people cannot be expected to have large personal resources, but they do want them to demonstrate their commitment. If the enterprise prospers, and eventually floats on the market or is sold on to another company, both the founders and their backers stand to make substantial capital gains.

Some successful start-ups are launched by a team of managers who worked together in an established company and decided to leave and use their skills to found a new business.

Management buy-out (MBO)

Many MBOs arise because a large group wishes to divest itself of a subsidiary, and selling to the management team is seen as a better option than selling to another company. Others take place when a family business is to be sold because the owner retires.

Incumbent managers are, or ought to be, better qualified than anyone else to know the potential value of the business they have been running. They also ought to be more aware than anyone else of the weaknesses of the business as well as its strengths, and their plans can take account of those weaknesses. Trade buyers, on the other hand, have to allow for the possibility of skeletons in the cupboard when they formulate their bid.

The ownership structure of a company after a buy-out varies according to circumstances. In a small MBO it is often possible for the managers to acquire the majority of the equity, even though they may be able to raise only a small proportion of the full purchase price out of their own resources. If they can subscribe enough capital to acquire, say, 65 per cent of the equity the venture capital backer subscribes the remaining 35 per cent, and also provides other forms of capital to meet the total requirement.

In a larger MBO, it is unrealistic for the managers to have a majority of the equity, but they will acquire a significant minority to provide an appropriate incentive. The remainder of the equity shares will be divided among one or more venture capital institutions.

Management buy-in (MBI)

A management buy-in is a variant of the MBO where a new management comes in from outside. The incoming managing director may bring his own team with him, or he may involve some members of the existing team in the new ownership structure, in which case it becomes a buy-in-management-buy-out (sometimes called a BIMBO).

Growth capital, development capital

Most business growth tends to be financed by debt, but there are situations where the extent of the project, or the risks involved, mean an injection of equity capital is necessary. This strengthens the balance sheet, and can make it easier to approach lenders to supply any necessary debt.

In some cases, of course, a company planning substantial growth may decide it is time to go for a quote on the stock market. It is useful to know that venture capital can sometimes provide an alternative to flotation.

In the case of a family business or a business owned by its management the notion of bringing in outside equity often requires a psychological breakthrough, but at the end of the day they may decide that it is better to own, say, 70 per cent of a soundly financed business rather than to be 100 per cent owners of a business which is unable to fulfil its full promise.

Obviously it is important for the management to find an investor whose ambitions are in line with their own.

Private placings

Another venture capital 'product' is the private placing. This simply means that an institutional investor acquires shares from an existing shareholder in a private company. It is an arrangement which can resolve various situations where – if the company were quoted – the shareholder could dispose of the shares on the stock market.

A common use of private placings is where a shareholder in a family company wishes to retire and other shareholders do not wish to acquire the shares.

Which sectors?

Venture capital has applications in almost all business sectors, but different circumstances will be addressed in different ways in the financial structuring of the deal. In a cash-generative business it may be appropriate to gear up an equity investment with substantial loan capital, because the business can service the debt. In the case of many young hi-tech and bio-tech businesses, profits will not emerge for several years and the investment will take the form wholly of equity.

The investor normally hopes to receive his reward in the form of capital gains if the business develops into a successful company and is taken over or floats.

Horses for courses

Companies providing venture capital vary enormously. Some specialise in hi-tech start-ups. Others are interested only in very large buy-outs and buy-ins. If you are in search of capital you should be aware of three specific respects in which suppliers of venture capital differ. Some are more 'hands on' than others, and may wish, for instance, to appoint one of their executives to the board of your company. The other difference is that, while some suppliers of venture capital are investing their own money, others are managers of funds raised from other sources, and are subject to the wishes of those who have put up the money. In particular, they may insist on an 'exit' from the investment within a fairly short timespan. Other investors are more flexible.

A third difference is that venture capitalists will normally have different minimum deal sizes below which they will not be interested to invest. For example, the majority will not look at any deal that is less than £1m, whilst others put the bar much higher still.

For businesses seeking smaller amounts of investment, say anything up to £1m, there has been the emergence of business angels and seed funds. Business angels are individuals or a group of individuals who risk their own money and invest at the very early stages of a company's development. Seed funds are companies that raise money, sometimes from wealthy individuals but often from venture capital companies or other organisations, and invest these smaller amounts at what is called the 'seed' stage of a company's development.

What does a venture capital company look for?

There is an old saying that only three things matter when an investor is deciding whether to back a project – people, people and people. Investors of venture capital reach their decisions very largely on the calibre of the management team they are being asked to back.

When you approach a venture capital company, the sector in which you operate is less important than your management qualities. Investors know that some of the best investments have been made in 'unfashionable' sectors, because there is always scope for the well-managed business which can buck the trend.

In approaching venture capital investors you should realise that they are probably looking for:

- A balanced management team, rather than a single individual, however talented. But there will usually be a clear leader.
- A team with a good track record – references will be taken up – and collectively must be able to exercise strong financial control.
- Managers with an entrepreneurial edge – they will be determined to make a success of the business. At the same time there should be a high level of managerial professionalism, possibly acquired by working as an executive in a large organisation before moving on to run a smaller company.

Sometimes, if investors like the basic growth plan, they may nevertheless feel the management team needs to be strengthened. This need not mean imposing the investor's nominee on the board. So far as 3i is concerned, a management-owned business is more likely to grow strongly when the managers know that the responsibility rests firmly in their hands. We are often able, however, to suggest names of appropriate independent non-executive directors whom executive directors would welcome to complement their skills.

When you approach a venture capital investor you will be expected to have a clear strategy and to have researched your growth plans thoroughly. There is little point in reproducing products already in ample supply. Do you have a sustainable competitive advantage? Have you identified a niche, or a USP?

Potential backers will also ask questions designed to establish whether you have the skills and experience required – plus an entrepreneurial urge and a determination to make the business grow.

Your answers will help them decide whether to back you, and if so on what terms. At the end of the day they, like you, expect a reasonable return on capital, having regard to the realities and the risks.

Do you have a clear view of where you rank in the market? Have you assessed what competitors will do when you implement your growth plan? They may react aggressively.

Can you explain your plans clearly to prospective backers, no matter how complicated technically your product may be? This is more than a courtesy. If you cannot describe the impact of your product in layman's terms, it may indicate that your have thought through your strategy less clearly than you imagined.

How much money is needed? How much will be provided from the managers' own resources?

Crises are bound to crop up as you develop your growth strategy. Can you demonstrate that you have thought through what happens then, and that you and your team are equipped to deal with problems? What results are you forecasting for sales, gross margins, profits and working capital, and what assumptions have been built into those forecasts? What about relations with customers and other business partners? Investors may wish to approach some of them for references. Do they agree with your assessment of your position, or potential position, in the marketplace? After all, if a business has let down a customer, it may let down investors too. Do your plans stand up to a 'sanity check' – have you stood back and asked the simple question, how sensible is this?

Venture capital as an instrument of restructuring

As we enter the 21st century, a powerful force in the reshaping of industry will continue to be that companies focus on their core business. Sometimes this occurs under external pressure, when a large organisation is forced to sell off a subsidiary in order to reduce its borrowings. But divestment also takes place as part of strategic planning, designed to secure maximum shareholder value by concentrating on those activities which the organisation does best.

The traditional form of divestment is a trade sale to another company. Recently, however, nearly half of the mergers and acquisitions market has consisted of management buy-outs and buy-ins. The initiative in this kind of restructuring has been taken by the venture capital industry itself. An institutional investor or venture capital fund will negotiate, for instance, with the vendor on the terms of the buy-out. Having agreed on the price to be paid, the institution then involves the management team of its own choice.

Vendors of businesses – whether plcs or family businesses – obviously want to be confident that they are securing the best price. Increasingly it is recognised in the M&A market that it makes sense, during the processes leading up to the sale, for vendors to conduct negotiations not only with potential trade buyers but with selected financial institutions which would be in a position to back an appropriate management team. Such institutions have the financial muscle to present highly credible proposals to vendors at a very early stage.

The professionalism of an experienced investment institution makes it possible to price businesses realistically and thus to match or exceed competitive bids.

A working relationship

As in all business relationships, it is good if the business and its venture capital backers feel that they are on the same side. It is a relationship which is going to continue for some years, and will almost certainly have to weather ups and downs. The two sides should be able to talk through the problems sensibly. At some stage you may have to raise another tranche of capital and must feel that you will have a sympathetic ear. Ideally, when you and a provider of venture capital, enter into a deal, you should feel that you are talking the same language.

7.2

Management Consultancy

Sarah Taylor,
MCA

The UK consultancy market

The world-wide market for management consultancy is currently worth $100 billion, having grown from less than $10 billion over the last decade. Approximately one tenth of that work is generated by UK-based consultancy firms, many of which are the European offshoots of large US firms, sometimes also servicing the Middle East and African regions. Most of those firms are based in London due to its growing status as a European centre for finance, technology and media.

The consultancy industry is a major contributor to the UK economy, representing 0.78 per cent of gross domestic product (GDP) compared to just 0.5 per cent in the US and an average of 0.4 per cent across Europe. In 2000 UK consultancy firms generated £1 billion of income from other countries.

The UK and Germany are by far the largest markets in Europe, representing 25.8 per cent and 28.6 per cent respectively. In third place, France represents just 17 per cent of the total European market. UK consultancy income is still showing above average growth for Europe at 21 per cent and market projections for 2001 are in the region of £8 billion.

Over half of the consultancy work done by UK-based firms is IT related (IT consultancy, systems integration or outsourcing) and nearly one third is in the financial services sector.

Management consultancy is, without doubt, one of the fastest growing areas of the UK economy. In the last five years, members of the Management Consultancies Association (MCA) have seen their revenues treble to £3.7 billion in 2000, with projections for 2001 at around £4 billion. Consultancy work in the financial services sector generated over £1 billion in 2000. While there was a drop off in IT

consultancy revenues due to the completion of Y2K and EMU compliance, IT work still represents over half of UK fee income and e-business
related consultancy is now estimated at 70 per cent. As it is normally
considered that MCA members account for approximately 50 per cent
of the consultancy revenues in the UK, this implies that the total market
for UK consultancy is in the region of £7 billion.

Management consultants offer an increasingly wide variety of services from mainstream strategic and IT consultancy to project management, marketing and more recently 'e-consulting'. This can sometimes
lead to problems with defining the scope and role of management
consultancy. Unlike the law and accounting professions, the industry is
unregulated and is sometimes portrayed unfairly by the media as secre-
tive and unaccountable.

The fact that over 90 per cent of the FTSE 100 use member firms of
the Association on a repeat basis, and continue to do so in ever increasing numbers, would indicate that consultancy firms, in the vast majority
of cases, give excellent value for money. This widespread use of
consultants is also reflected in the public sector.

How do consultancy firms differ?

The consultancy industry is currently undergoing dramatic change in
response to regulatory pressures and the growth of the digital economy.
Until recently, practices could be divided into four main types: general-
ist, strategy, HR and IT. A number of new players have recently entered
the market such as the e-consultancies and this is causing the more
traditional players to rethink their services, structures and finance.

Generalist

These are the largest firms in the UK and offer a wide range of services
from strategy consulting to human resources and IT on a global basis.
They include such well known names as Accenture (formerly
Andersen Consulting), PricewaterhouseCoopers and PA Consulting.
Clients often establish long-term relationships with these consultancies making use of different services at different stages of their development. Many of these practices grew out of the Big Five accountancy
firms and are now under pressure to demonstrate their independence
from the audit side of the business as well as to attract and retain the
best talent.

Strategy consulting

Within this category are firms like McKinsey and Arthur D Little. Smaller than the generalists, the majority of these organisations are American. As the term suggests they primarily offer strategic advice to companies on a project by project basis. As the networked economy develops, they too are recruiting e-business experts and moving into investment and incubation of new ventures. In 2000 corporate strategy work represented 16 per cent of MCA revenues.

Human resource consulting

These firms offer specialist advice ranging from reviews of salaries and benefits to development of leadership skills. They include organisations like Hay Management Consultants and Towers Perrin.

IT consulting

With the massive growth in IT consulting and systems spending by companies in the 1990s, former systems development and hardware specialists in this field saw the attractions of offering more mainstream consulting advice. Within this group are IBM Consulting Group, CSC Computer Sciences Corporation and CMG. Over the 24 months to December 31 2000, spend on IT consultancy increased by 63 per cent.

E-consulting

Many of the large consultancy firms now estimate that up to 70 per cent of their income is e-business-related. Since 1997, wider web access and better technology has driven the development of e-business at a frantic pace. Clients are looking for help with their e-strategies and implementation. Much of the recent work in this area has been with the more established 'bricks and mortar' organisations that are now recognising the opportunities offered by the Internet.

In 2000, a number of pure Internet consultancies emerged such as Scient, Viant and Sapient, many transferring skills, experience and staff from the States where the e-consultancy market was more mature. These firms had to grow at a phenomenal rate to keep pace with client demand, often luring consultants away from the more traditional firms with offers of share options and flexible working. More recently these new consultancies have suffered from the economic downturn and some have had to downscale their operations.

The more traditional consultancies recruited large numbers of e-business specialists and some launched their own e-business brands such as Roundarch (Deloitte and WPP) and Metrius (KPMG Consulting).

Many firms have become key players in the economy through their incubator and venture capital activities eg Accenture (formerly Andersen Consulting), Mckinsey and Bain all have incubators which develop and launch dot.com start-ups, often providing consultancy in exchange for equity. Accenture's 'e-units' allow staff to share in the wealth created by AC's venture capital operations around the world.

Recent developments in UK consultancy industry

Over the last ten years, IT decisions have moved from the backroom to the boardroom as technology has become a key business driver. There is no longer such a thing as a pure IT project or a pure strategy project. Clients are demanding 'end-to end' solutions combining management consultancy and systems integration. Technology has enabled clients to operate on a global basis and their consultants have had to match their global reach.

Enterprise Resource Planning (ERP) was the first major IT investment for many large corporations. The need for Y2K compliance provided an extra impetus for ERP as organisations chose to invest in ERP rather than modify their existing systems. Consultants had a key role to play in ensuring that business processes were appropriately re-engineered and that those within the organisation supported and implemented the changes.

Another phenomenon of the last ten years has been the massive growth in the outsourcing industry ie the delivery of non-core services (usually IT) by a third party organisation. Here again, management consultants can make the difference between a highly successful outsoucing contract and one which delivers little value.

In the last couple of years there has been a marked shift in emphasis from IT projects which reduce costs to those which add value such as Customer Relationship Management, salesforce automation, knowledge management and collaborative commerce.

Many clients have also learned from their first experiences of ERP or outsourcing that consultancy support is needed to get maximum return on investment using change management, process re-engineering and communications. Enterprise Application Integration (EAI), will remove the need for large and costly systems integration projects and will enable modifications to be made more quickly and cost effectively. There will be more choice and flexibility for the customer but it will become even more important to stay one step ahead of the competition. The role for consultants is to ensure that the right products are used for each organisation and that products can be replaced or updated according to changing circumstances.

The growth in business to business (B2B) activity has been identified as a major trend for the next five years in the UK. Internet-based software will encourage the growth of collaborative commerce, e-procurement, digital market places and supply chain management.

As clients look for integrated solutions to their management and IT requirements, many consultancy firms are entering into alliances with software suppliers, telcos or communications conglomerates in order to provide a broader range of services to their clients and to extend their global reach. For example, Cisco has a 20 per cent stake in KPMG Consulting; last year Cap Gemini purchased the consultancy arm of Ernst & Young and is now launching a global telecoms consultancy firm with Cisco. Deloitte is working with WPP to provide e-marketing solutions through Roundarch.

The audit-based consultancy firms such as KPMG and PricewaterhouseCoopers are being closely scrutinised by the US Securities and Exchange Commission which has increased controls on the consultancy work provided by audit firms to their clients. One response is to float the consultancy business. KPMG Consulting and Accenture have already launched Initial Public Offerings and PricewaterhouseCoopers may follow. Flotation also provides the opportunity to access money markets for the much needed capital for expansion and in the 'war for talent', stock options are becoming a powerful weapon. However, opinion in the industry is divided on flotations and a variety of other solutions to the problems of SEC control and the need for capital are emerging.

The boundaries between different types of consultants and even between consultants and suppliers are becoming increasingly blurred as the strategy houses move into e-business implementation and the software suppliers offer strategic advice. With clients struggling to keep pace with technological change the opportunities for consultancy services are numerous. There is, however, evidence that the economic downturn in the US is having an impact on the European economies, which in turn is slowing growth in the consultancy sector.

The war for talent remains an issue with consultancy firms competing for specialist skills. In response, many of the more traditional firms are having to rethink their whole structure. Young high fliers want and expect to become partners sooner and to share in the profits. In-house incubators offer employees the chance to develop their creative and entrepreneurial skills within the security of a large firm. AT Kearney even allows consultants time off to work on their own e-enterprises. Staff bonuses are sometimes linked to the performance of these

ventures, providing a further incentive to stay with the firm. The traditional partnership structure is also being reviewed in order to offer more
consultants a share of the profits at an earlier stage in their career.

Whilst firms are reporting higher staff retention rates than 12 months
ago, there is always a need to recruit those with the right mix of skills to
meet client demand. London-based firms have access to a large pool of
highly qualified, experienced and mobile consultants and the UK boasts
some of the top business schools in Europe. European consultants
generally have more experience of working across borders; of different
cultures, legislations and languages. They relish the challenges of
managing pan-European and global teams and are happy to be moved
around Europe at short notice.

Changing relationships with clients and competitors

Increasingly, management consultancy firms are becoming directly
involved in the economy rather than simply enabling it to function
effectively. Their cross industry contacts and experience place them at
the heart of the new business networks or 'ecosystems'. Their investment of time and money in new ventures is actually fuelling the growth
of e-business. Their multiple alliances with software and telco vendors
is extending their influence and changing the nature of their relationships with their clients. Management consultancies seem to be perme-
ating all areas of the networked economy and setting trends for new
ways of working both within their own organisations and across whole
industry sectors.

The increasing importance of networks in the new economy is
having a major impact on the role of the consultancy firm. Rather than
simply advising their clients, they are now initiating alliances between
or with clients, investing in or purchasing clients or incubating new
ventures. They are becoming key players and active participants in the
economy. The new breed of consultant will be more flexible and entrepreneurial than their old economy counterparts, allowing strategy to be
constantly modified and objectives re-evaluated .

At the same time the consultant/client relationship is changing. The
boundaries are blurring. Consultants can become part of the client
organisation for periods of time, may invest in them and ultimately
share in their profits. Consultancy firms which have historically
competed are now working together on client projects. There will be
greater convergence within and outside the industry as firms co-operate
and merge in order to better service their clients. Convergence has been
a particularly strong trend in the UK as firms seek economies of scale
and critical mass through mergers, acquisitions and joint ventures.

Venture consulting will increase as consultancies use their networks and skills to identify and nurture business opportunities. This will also provide those firms with a means of attracting and retaining their best people, allowing them to develop and use entrepreneurial skills in the security of a large firm.

London provides an environment which is particularly conducive to networking and enterprise. Many multinationals have their European, Middle East and Africa bases in London; it is the European centre for advertising, communications, media and finance. It is a truly multicultural, international centre with a highly skilled and mobile workforce. And as long as management consultancy relies on highly skilled individuals, entrepreneurial flair and extensive networks, London will remain the largest concentration of management consultancy firms outside the States.

How to choose a consultancy

In a recent survey by the MCA we asked clients why they had chosen to use a member firm. The following key themes emerged:

- the consultancy firm employed had skills or knowledge that the client lacked;
- the consultancy was able to offer an independent view of the problem;
- the consultancy was able to offer some original thinking;
- the consultancy was able to facilitate and stimulate internal debate.

Consultancies were used because they supplemented a company's existing resources. They were seen as offering additional skills or knowledge and providing independent advice, or generating outside, original thinking. Consultancies were viewed as supporting but not replacing existing management resources; as working in partnership with their client.

The underlying factor behind the decision to use a consultancy was to supplement their existing management skills or knowledge. Consultants can draw on a vast reservoir of often global knowledge and experience to approach a problem with a fresh opinion and an external viewpoint.

There are also situations when it is not appropriate to use a consultant. For example, to confirm a management decision that has already been made or in order to deflect blame onto the consultants. Clients must also take responsibility for briefing their consultants and keeping them informed. It is difficult for consultants to offer sound advice without all the appropriate information or when the client is unclear about their own objectives.

How to use a consultancy

The most effective consultancy projects are those in which client and consultant work as members of a team, each bringing their own knowledge, expertise and resources to bear in realising an opportunity or resolving a problem. Team members who trust one another will share information and knowledge and, as a result, work together effectively and efficiently. Getting the commercial relationship between client and consultant right is essential in establishing this kind of trust.

The MCA has developed a Statement of Best Practice in conjunction with HM Treasury and the Institute of Management Consultancy. The document provides practical advice on project definition, consultancy selection, contract terms, project management and evaluation. Primarily aimed at public sector users of consultancy the principles apply to all client-consultant relationships. Here are some examples of the advice offered to clients;

- Do not be afraid of providing too much information to your consultants who prefer this to a lack of detail.
- The briefing for the consultants should contain information about the project and the people involved, and should outline broad criteria used at the selection of bidder and evaluation of tender stage.
- Build in the expected outputs from the project and any budgetary constraints which the business case has highlighted.
- On appointment, confirm with a written statement the key elements of the way the project will be carried out, to include a plan, deliverables and expectations. This should also contain a risk register defining who is responsible for which risks.
- Flag up problems with the project early on so that remedial action can be implemented.
- Hold regular reviews on the progress and delivery of the contract and project. Action points arising from review meetings should be agreed in writing.
- Where necessary and agreed, provide staff, facilities and information promptly.
- At the end of the project both parties should undertake a joint project review to see what they might gain from the experience.

Many clients rely on word-of-mouth recommendations when selecting a consultancy. Whilst this is an important element of the process, every organisation will have different requirements of a consultancy and the client-consultant 'chemistry' can vary enormously according to the culture of the two organisations.

The MCA would suggest a combination of personal recommendation and a more structured approach to consultancy selection. We are able to provide detailed information on our member firms, what they do and the types of clients they have worked with in the past.

Copies of The Statement of Best Practice are available from MCA. Tel 020 7321 3990, email mca@mca.org.uk, web-site: www.mca.org.uk

Part 8

Education

8.1

Schools Provision

Ruth Stedman, ISCis

Relocating is a stressful affair, but even more so if you are bringing your family with you. How do you go about finding the right schools for your children? What different types of schools are there? How easy is it to get a place?

The British Education System

When it comes to education, parents in Britain have a choice: they can send their child to a state (maintained) school, as is their entitlement by law, or they can choose to send their child to an independent (private or fee-paying school). The Department for Education and Skills (DfES www.dfes.gov.uk) and the Local Education Authorities (LEAs) can provide you with information about the state education provision in each area. However, if you are considering an independent school, ISCis (Independent Schools Council information service) can help.

What is an independent school? Essentially it is a fee-charging school which has the freedom to develop its own curriculum and ethos. There are over 2400 in the UK educating over 600,000 children. 1300 of them are accredited to the Independent Schools Council (ISC). ISIS is the information arm of the ISC.

All independent schools must be registered with the DfES. All ISCis schools, through membership of the ISC, will be subject to inspection by the Independent Schools Inspectorate (ISI). ISI has formal government approval and has replaced Ofsted (Office for Standards in Education) as the agency advising the DfES on whether schools are meeting statutory requirements. Schools are now inspected every six years.

Schools that are not accredited to ISC may choose so for a number of reasons and are not necessarily poor schools. However, the 2000 Annual Report by Her Majesty's Chief Inspector of Schools commented that, 'overall, schools in the ISC perform substantially better than schools outside its membership.'
Independent schools are not required by law to follow the National Curriculum as schools in the state system are. Nonetheless, a majority of independent schools follow the basic progression of the National Curriculum, ending with GCSEs and the new AS/A2 levels (which have replaced the A-level) – the passport into university.

But an independent school's curriculum extends well beyond the minimum requirements of the National Curriculum. Independent schools spend more time on music, arts, sports and tend to introduce languages and sciences at a younger age. Some prep (junior) independent schools enter their pupils in the national Key Stage Tests and those that do are normally happy to release their results. Overall, based on those prep schools that sit the tests, the results are consistently well above the national averages.

Independent senior schools prepare pupils for GCSE and A-Level exams. Many have particular strengths, such as sciences or art. Results in the independent sector are good. In 2000, over 50 per cent of independent school entries achieved an A* or A, compared to 15.8 per cent nationally. At A-level, 60 per cent of entries scored either an A or B, markedly higher than the 37 per cent nationally.

Subject choices at GCSE and A-level are varied, from the traditional languages, arts and sciences to Chinese, Music Technology, Dance and Classical Civilisation. Many schools are also pioneering developments in Information Technology with some now using interactive whiteboards in classrooms and others encouraging pupils to use laptops in their lessons.

Choosing an independent school

What type of school would your child thrive in? Large or small? Would you prefer your child to go to a single-sex or co-educational school? There are benefits in both type of school and often the choice rests on what you think would be best for your child.

Would you prefer a day or a boarding school or one that offers both? Day schools in London are amongst the most heavily oversubscribed and if you are prepared to consider a boarding school you may find there is a wider choice available to you. To help families where both parents work, many boarding schools now offer an extended day or flexible / weekly boarding provision. Many children enjoy being part of a boarding community with the huge range of extra-curricular activities and fantastic facilities. If you haven't considered a boarding school before, it may be worth visiting just to see what is on offer.

Unlike in the state sector, many independent schools take pupils from nursery age right through to age eighteen. This saves switching from a nursery to a prep (junior) school to a senior school, but many parents prefer their child to experience at least one change of school.

Some independent schools are very academically selective. Others accept pupils with a wide range of academic abilities. Each school's selection process will have a profound effect on pupil performance in national tests and performance tables.

Many parents call ISCis asking about the importance of 'League Tables'. By all means look at them but bear in mind that many of the schools at the top of the tables are selecting the brightest children using rigorous testing and assessment prior to entry – so you would expect them to do very well in the tables. However, for larger, selective schools the tables can indicate consistency in achievement as well as improvement over, say, a five-year period.

Although a significant proportion of pupils in independent schools are very academic, there are also those who achieve good grades above and beyond any initial expectation when the child first entered the school. This is what schools refer to sometimes as the 'added value' and it is something many independent schools provide through small class sizes, excellent resources and specialist teaching support.
Nonetheless it is important to be reassured that every school, selective or not, has the academic rigour to support bright pupils. One of the best ways of assessing this is to ask where schools are sending their pupils on to. Prep schools should have a wide range of senior schools that they feed pupils into, showing that they have the resources to support individual children's needs and abilities. Senior schools should be sending pupils on to a wide range of universities to read everything from History to Hotel and Tourism, Mathematics to Business Studies, Engineering to Computing.

Drawing up a shortlist of schools

Schools in London and the South East of England are often oversubscribed and it helps if you can be flexible about where you are going to live. Once you have decided on areas you may live and what your basic requirements are, you need to look at which schools match your needs and draw up a shortlist.

If you are specifically looking for a school in London or the South East of England, your first step should be to consult our website www.isis.uk.net/southeast or telephone our office 020 7798 1560 to request a free regional guide. In it you will not only find details of over

530 schools in London and the South-East but also lots of useful information on how to find the right school for your child.

When you have several schools in mind, contact them and ask for their prospectus – or look at their website (if they have one). Both should give you more insight into each school's ethos, academic performance, range of extra-curricular activities and facilities.

However, to get a real taste of what any school is like you should visit. Most schools have Open Days at certain times of the year providing a good opportunity for a first look, but you should also see your shortlisted schools when they are operating normally with lessons in progress.

Try to meet the Head and have some questions ready to ask. For example, what is the school's policy on discipline and bullying? Does the Head seem motivated and passionate about the school? Heads play a very important part in shaping the atmosphere of the school and it is vital that you feel happy about leaving your child in their care. Look at the children in the schools. Do they seem happy and busy? Is there a good rapport between staff and pupils? Talk to pupils. Ask them what they like about their school and what they don't like.

You also need to check with each school what its registration, admissions and testing procedures are. Some schools, especially those for younger children work on a 'first come, first served' basis and others expect high academic standards. Assess your child's capabilities and interests. Would a highly selective school, where competition is fierce, be the right choice for your child? Many able children perform just as well in a school that has pupils across all ability ranges.

Once you have registered at a school you then need to prepare your child for any selection tests or interviews. Registration does not guarantee a place. Only the assessment can do this. If your child is successful then a formal offer of a place will be made. Most schools hold their entrance tests in January so the more time you have to choose schools the better. If you are looking for an immediate place then if you find a school that does have a vacancy they may test your child either at the school, or make arrangements with their present school overseas. Few schools will accept pupils over the age of four without having met either the parents or child and without some form of assessment. Sometimes schools can arrange for tests to be sat in the child's present school but you should expect to have to visit your shortlisted schools.

ISCis is here to help you

Choosing the right school for your child is one of the most important decisions you can make. Over half of all parents choosing independent schools are first-time buyers, where neither parent attended an independent school. And if you are also moving from abroad you might be unsure of how our school system works. This can make the task even more daunting. If you are finding the whole process confusing or need immediate advice London and South East ISCis is here to help.

Our staff are happy to help, not only with advising and providing basic information, but also to offer consultation services for companies and families to narrow the choice and even find places in the region's schools. Details about our various services can be found in the handbook.

If your child is currently at an International School then there are several in ISCis membership. If you are happy with your child's present schooling you may feel a similar type of school may be most suitable. More and more independent schools offer the International Baccalaureate and you can find out about these and international schools from ISCis.

Whatever your specific needs and requirements there will be an ISCis school for you and your family. It may take some time to find a place, but all our schools are sympathetic and are as accommodating as possible to those moving here from abroad.

And don't forget that ISCis either by telephone, in person or on the world wide web, is here to help.

Appendices

Appendix 1
Contributors' Details

3i
91 Waterloo Road
London SE1 8XP
Tel: +44 (0)20 7928 3131
Fax: +44 (0)20 7928 0058
Web: www.3i.com

The Bank of England
Tel: +44 (0)20 7601 4411
Fax: +44 (0)20 7601 5460
Email: press@bankofengland.co.uk

BKR Haines Watts
13 Hanover Square
London W1S 1JS
Tel: +44 (0)20 7495 5544
Fax: +44 (0)20 7495 7722

Corporation of London
PO Box 270
Guildhall
London EC2P 2EJ
Tel: +44 (0)20 7606 3030
Fax: +44 (0)20 7332 1119
Web: www.cityoflondon.gov.uk

DHL
Tel: (0)20 8818 8049
Fax: (0)20 8818 8581
Email: jhurley@lhr-co.gb.dhl.com

DLA
3 Noble Street
London EX2V 7EE
Tel: +44 (0)20 7796 6619
Fax: +44 (0)20 7600 1738
Email: jonathan.exten-wright@dla.com
Web: www.dla.com

Houston Consulting Europe
Tel: +32 2504 8044
Fax: +32 2504 8050
Web: www.houston-consulting.com

ISIS London and South East
Grosvenor Gardens House
35–37 Grosvenor Gardens
London SW1W 0BS
Tel: +44 (0)20 7798 1560
Fax: +44 (0)20 7798 1562
Email: southeast@isis.org.uk
Web: www.isis.org.uk/southeast

King Sturge
7 Stratford Place
London W1C 1ST
Tel: +44 (0)20 7529 6894
Fax: +44 (0)20 7409 1135

London Chamber of Commerce & Industry
33 Queen Street
London EC4R 1AP
Tel: +44 (0)20 7203 1889
Fax: +44 (0)20 7203 1930

London First Centre
Tel: +44 (0)20 7665 1508
Fax: +44 (0)20 7925 2022
Email: acooke@lfc.co.uk
Web: www.lfc.co.uk

Management Consultancies Association (MCA)
Suite 3 2nd Floor
49 Whitehall
London SW1A 2EX
Tel: +44 (0)20 7321 3990
Fax: +44 (0)20 7321 3991
Email: mca@mca.org.uk
Web: www.mca.org.uk

Manpower PLC
International House
66 Chiltern Street
London W1U 4JT
Tel: +44 (0)20 7224 6688
Fax: +44 (0)20 7224 5253
Email: keith.Faulkner@manpower.co.uk
Web: www.manpower.co.uk

Salt
Hyde Park House
5 Manfred Road
London SW15 2RS
Tel: +44 (0)20 8870 6777
Fax: +44 (0)20 8874 2150

Appendix 2
Overseas Chambers in the UK

ARAB STATES
Arab-British Chamber of Commerce

6 Belgrave Square
LONDON
SW1
Great Britain

Mr Abdul Karim Al-Mudaris
Secretary General
Tel: 020 7235 4363
Fax: 020 7201 9408

ARGENTINA
British-Argentine Chamber of Commerce

2 Belgrave Square
LONDON
SW1X 8PJ
Great Britain

Mr Michael Cannon
Tel: 020 7245 6661
Fax: 020 7235 7013

AUSTRALIA
Australian/New Zealand Chamber of Commerce

5th Floor
Queensland House
393 Strand
LONDON
WC2R 0LT
Great Britain

Mr Gordon Scott
Director
Tel: 020 7379 0720
Fax: 020 7379 0721

BANGLADESH
Bangladesh British Chamber of Commerce

7-15 Greatorex Street
LONDON
E1 5NF

Tel: 020 7247 5525

BELGIUM
Belgium Luxembourg Chamber of Commerce
Berkeley House
2nd Floor
73 Upper Richmond Road
LONDON
SW15 2SZ
Great Britain

Miss Dominique Maeremans
Tel: 020 8877 3025
Fax: 0201 8877 3961

BRAZIL
Brazilian Chamber of Commerce in Great Britain
32 Green Street
LONDON
W1Y 3FD
Great Britain

Mr Dionisio Augusto De Castro Cerqueira
Tel: 020 7499 0186
Fax: 020 7493 5105
E-Mail:dionisio@infolondres.org.uk

CANADA
Canada-UK Chamber of Commerce
38 Grosvenor Street
LONDON
W1X 0DP
Great Britain

Mr Michael Hall
Tel: 020 7258 6576
Fax: 020 7258 6594

CARIBBEAN
The British-Caribbean Chamber of Commerce
34-38 Beverley Road
HULL
HU3 1YE
Great Britain

Mr Ian Kelly
Tel: 01482 324976
Fax: 01482 213962

CHILE
British Chilean Chamber of Commerce
12 Devonshire Street
LONDON
W1N 2DS
Great Britain

Mrs Sandra Carey
Tel: 020 7323 3053
Fax: 020 7436 5204

DENMARK
The Danish-UK Chamber of Commerce
55 Sloane Street
Royal Danish Embassy
LONDON
SW1X 9SR
Great Britain

Mr Ole Hviid Jensen
Tel: 020 7259 6795
Fax: 020 7823 1200

EGYPT
Egyptian-British Chamber of Commerce
299 Oxford St   Tel: 020 7499 3100
LONDON
W1C 2DZ

FRANCE
French Chamber of Commerce in Great Britain
21 Dartmouth Street   Ms Pam Duffin
LONDON   Tel: 020 7304 4040
SW14 9PB   Fax: 020 7304 7034
Great Britain

GERMANY
German-British Chamber of Industry and Commerce
Mecklenburg House   Mr Ulrich Hoppe
16 Buckingham Gate   Tel: 020 7976 4100
LONDON   Fax: 020 7976 4101
SW1E 6LB
Great Britain

IRAN
The British-Iranian Chamber of Commerce
Chichester House   The Viscount Waverley
278-282 High Holborn   Chairman
LONDON   Tel: 020 7405 4868
WC1V 7HA   Fax: 020 7405 4869
Great Britain   E-Mail: bicoc@aol.com

ISRAEL
British-Israel Chamber of Commerce
Canada House   Mr Brian Cohen
272 Fieldend Road   Tel: 020 8582 0485
Eastcote, RUISLIP   Fax: 020 8582 0486
Middlesex HA4 9NA
Great Britain

ITALY
Italian Chamber of Commerce for Great Britain
1 Princes Street   Mr Barry Walker
LONDON   Tel: 020 7495 8191
W1R 8AY   Fax: 020 7495 8194
Great Britain

JAPAN
Japanese Chamber of Commerce & Industry
Rooms 493-495   Mr Akira Wakasugi
2nd Floor   Tel: 020 7628 0069
Salisbury House   Fax: 020 7628 0248
29 Finsbury Circus
LONDON
EC2M 5QQ
Great Britain

NETHERLANDS
Netherland-British Chamber of Commerce
The Dutch House   Mr Willem P Offenberg
307-308 High Holborn   Deputy Director
LONDON   Tel: 020 7242 1064
WC1V 7LS   Fax: 020 7831 4831
Great Britain

NORWAY
Norwegian-British Chamber of Commerce
Charles House   Mrs Inger-Marie Cawley
5 Lower Regent Street   Tel: 020 7930 0181
LONDON   Fax: 020 7930 7946
SW1Y 4LR
Great Britain

POLAND
British-Polish Chamber of Commerce
55 Princes Gate   Tel: 020 7591 0057
Exhibition Road
LONDON
SW7 2PN

PORTUGAL
Portuguese UK Chamber of Commerce & Industry
Fourth Floor   Mr Ronnie A Price
22-25a Sackville Street   Director General
LONDON   Tel: 020 7494 1844
W1X 1DE   Fax: 020 7494 1822
Great Britain   E-Mail:info@portuguese-chamber.org.uk.

ROMANIA
British Romanian Chamber of Commerce

P O Box 367

509 Footscray Road

LONDON

SE9 3UJ

Great Britain

Mr Paul M Beza

Tel: 020 8302 0310

Fax: 020 8309 1321

E-Mail: BrittEng@compuserve.com

RUSSIA
Russo-British Chamber of Commerce

42 Southwark Street

LONDON

SE1 1UN

Great Britain

Mr David Cant

Tel: 020 7403 1706

Fax: 020 7403 1245

SPAIN
Spanish Chamber of Commerce in Great Britain

5 Cavendish Square

LONDON

W1M 0DP

Great Britain

Mr Jose Fernandez Bragado

Secretary General

Tel: 020 7637 9061

Fax: 020 7436 7188

SWEDEN
Swedish Chamber of Commerce

73 Welbeck Street

LONDON

W1M 7HA

Great Britain

Ms Ulla O'Barius

Tel: 020 7486 4545

Fax: 020 7935 5487

TURKEY
Turkish British Chamber of Commerce & Industry

Bury House

33 Bury Street

LONDON

SW1Y 6AU

Great Britain

Mr Barry Thorne

Tel: 020 7321 0999/0904

Fax: 020 7321 0989

UKRAINE
British Chamber of Commerce for the Ukraine

73 Cranmore Lane

ALDERSHOT

GU11 3AP

Great Britain

Mr Simon Hemans

Tel: 01252 312 296

Fax: 01252 337 352

UNITED STATES OF AMERICA
American Chamber of Commerce

75 Brook Street
LONDON
W1Y 2EB
Great Britain

Mr Robert Brunck
Tel: 020 7493 0381
Fax: 020 7493 2394

UNITED STATES OF AMERICA
British-American Chamber of Commerce

8 Staple Inn
Holborn
LONDON
WC1V 7QH
Great Britain

Mr Oliver Phillips
Tel: 020 7404 6400
Fax: 020 7404 6828
E-Mail: Info@bacc.co.uk

Appendix 3
Internet Site Addresses

Government Sites

www.europa.eu.int	EU official site
www.london.gov.uk	Greater London Authority site
www.open.gov.uk	portal to all UK Government sites
www.parliament.uk	Portal to House of Commons, House of Lords and Parliamentary sites

Business Organisations Sites

www.bankofengland.co.uk/	Bank of England – large statistics database
www.bba.org.uk/	British Bankers Association
www.cbi.org.uk	Confederation of British Industry site
www.fsb.co.uk	Federation of Small Businesses site
www.londonchamber.co.uk	London Chamber of Commerce and Industry site
www.londonstockexchange.com/	London Stock Exchange site
www.tuc.org.uk	Trade Unions Congress site

Business Information Sites

www.AccountingWEB.co.uk — accounting community umbrella site, many links and resources

www.companies-house.gov.uk — official site for company registration and investigation

www.ft.com — Financial Times homepage

http://www.icclaw.mainhost.co.uk/legal 500-series-lawyers-uk-law-journals-b.html — cumbersome address for legal 500 resource

www.inlandrevenue.gov.uk — official government tax and excise duty site

www.kogan-page.co.uk — Kogan Page Business Publishers site

http://www.marketing.strath.ac.uk/ — use their "Marketing Resources" section for excellent link page

www.thebiz.co.uk — business directories, events, conferences site

Miscellaneous Sites

www.thisislondon.co.uk/ — London Evening Standard's site, news & lifestyle pages

www.timeout.com — listings portal for London (and other cities)

www.foodferry.com — London's most established home delivery supermarket

Index of advertisers

10 128 BR 8022
FM
04/04 04-172-00 GBC